P9-DWC-378

3 2052 00453 5566

DISCARD

Collection Management

9/13 17-1 10/12

8/96 - 3
9/09 12(2) 12/03

APR 1992

Roald Amundsen, left
Robert Scott, above right

THE WORLD'S GREAT EXPLORERS

Roald Amundsen and Robert Scott

By Paul P. Sipiera

Consultant: Edward J. Olsen, Ph.D.,
Curator of Meteorites and Minerals,
Field Museum of Natural History,
Chicago, Illinois

CHILDRENS PRESS®

CHICAGO

Huskies at Scott Base, Antarctica

Opposite page:
Antarctic sea ice floating off Ross Island's Cape Evans

Dedication: To the memory of my parents, Paul and Frances

Project Editor: Ann Heinrichs
Designer: Lindaanne Donohoe
Cover Art: Steven Gaston Dobson
Engraver: Liberty Photoengraving

Copyright © 1990 by Childrens Press ®, Inc.
All rights reserved. Published simultaneously in Canada.
Printed in the United States of America.
1 2 3 4 5 6 7 8 9 10 R 99 98 97 96 95 94 93 92 91 90

Library of Congress Cataloging-in-Publication Data
Sipiera, Paul P.
  Roald Amundsen and Robert Scott / by Paul P. Sipiera.
    p. cm. — (The World's great explorers)
  Includes bibliographical references and index.
  Summary: Describes the competition between Roald Amundsen and Robert Scott to reach the South Pole, with emphasis on the personalities of the two explorers.
  ISBN 0-516-03056-6
    1. Scott, Robert Falcon, 1868-1912—Journeys—Juvenile literature. 2. Amundsen, Roald, 1872-1928—Journeys—Juvenile literature. 3. British Antarctic ("Terra Nova") Expedition (1910-1913)—Juvenile literature. 4. South Pole—Juvenile literature. [1. Amundsen, Roald, 1872-1928. 2. Scott, Robert Falcon, 1868-1912. 3. Explorers. 4. South Pole.] I. Title. II. Series.
G850 1910.S4S57 1990
919.8'9—dc20   90-2178
[B]   CIP
[920]   J 919.89   AC
          (B)

Table of Contents

Chapter 1
Introduction

Captain Robert Falcon Scott and his four followers had been advancing toward the South Pole for over seventy-seven days. They had endured many blizzards, crossed over the treacherous ice of the Beardmore Glacier, and were now suffering from malnutrition and vitamin deficiencies. They were mentally and physically exhausted. Yet, they pushed on toward an imaginary point that was their goal. They wanted to be the first men to stand at the South Pole. It was that desire alone that kept them going. All the hardships they had encountered would be forgotten once they reached the pole, and they were determined to make it.

In the late afternoon of January 17, 1912, something began to feel very wrong. After calculating that their position was very close to the pole, they noticed a curious black speck ahead of them on the horizon. For weeks these British explorers had known that they were in a race with a Norwegian team, but they never admitted to the possibility of losing to them. As they pushed on, the speck became a black flag fluttering in the wind. Then more and more signs of the Norwegians' presence told the story. Roald Amund-

A member of Amundsen's exploration party posing by the Norwegian flag they erected at the South Pole

sen and his companions had been the first to reach the South Pole. They made it there on December 14, 1911, over a month before Scott. The race was now lost, and all Scott could do was return home and report the news. He had failed.

Both Robert Scott and Roald Amundsen possessed the spirit of adventure that makes for a great explorer. Both men were very ambitious and determined to achieve greatness. Each wanted to secure for himself a lasting place of honor in the history of exploration. To achieve this end, they would have to succeed at some great feat, and they saw polar exploration as the best way to do this. However, although they shared a similar ambition, their individual personalities were very different. This basic difference would lead Amundsen to success and Scott to defeat.

Roald Amundsen seems to have been a man born for exploration. From his earliest days as a child, he had the desire to go to sea and visit distant lands. Very early in his career, he began to prepare for the day when he might lead his own expedition of discovery. When that day finally arrived, he was ready.

Amundsen was an explorer who believed in careful preparation before beginning any undertaking. First he would research everything that had been written on the area he planned to explore. Then he would interview as many people as possible who had already been there, to find out what they had learned. Amundsen would also test all of his equipment himself before deciding on what to take with him. Anything that proved unsatisfactory was redesigned or specially adapted to suit his needs. No detail was too small to be left to chance, and he learned well from the experiences of others.

In contrast to Amundsen, Robert Scott believed that success could always be achieved through hard work and determination alone. No obstacle was so great that he could not overcome it by the sheer force of his will. Because of this attitude, Scott paid much less attention to detail than Amundsen did. Instead of preparing for the worst possible conditions, Scott based his decisions on optimistic reports and better-than-average conditions. He left no room for the unexpected. Scott also let his personal feelings cloud his judgment. His decisions often went against the advice of more experienced people because of personality differences between them. This would one day prove fatal for Scott and for those who followed him to the South Pole.

For the explorers of the late nineteenth and early twentieth centuries, there were three prized goals of exploration. One was to be the first to make the Northwest Passage. This was the water route between the Atlantic and Pacific oceans through North America's Arctic waterways. The other two goals were to reach the North and South geographic poles. There was much curiosity about what could be found in the polar regions. Many people wanted to be the first to discover these wonders, and Amundsen and Scott were among them.

Before their well-publicized race to the South Pole, both Amundsen and Scott were successful explorers. Each was driven partly by personal ambition and partly by national pride. Although they would follow different directions in their explorations, the paths of Amundsen and Scott were destined to cross in Antarctica. But why Antarctica and the South Pole? For one reason, it was the only place left. Amundsen had

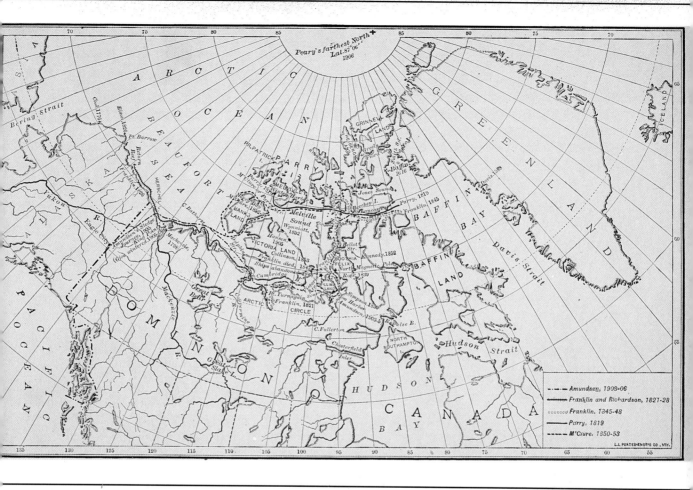

achieved the Northwest Passage in 1906, and Robert E. Peary had reached the North Pole in 1909. Only the South Pole remained as an unclaimed prize, and both Amundsen and Scott were determined to have it for their own.

Antarctica, because it lies so far from civilization, was regarded since earliest times as a land of mystery. So little was known about it that very few people even believed it existed. In fact, maps of the fifteenth century labeled the entire southern part of the earth as "fogs." Any land that might have been there was called *Terra Australis Incognita*—the Unknown Southern Land.

Map showing the routes that several explorers followed in search of the Northwest Passage

Greek philosophers from as early as 400 B.C. thought about the existence of a great southern continent that was covered by ice. This idea came from sailors' tales of a land of cold and ice that lay to the far north. They named this land *Arktikos*, after the star constellation of the Great Bear, Arctos. This constellation always appeared in the northern sky and seemed to turn around a single point. That point was later called the Arctic Pole. Because the Greeks believed in a balanced world, they pictured a second land to the south, where a point opposite the Arctic Pole would be found. This would later be called the Antarctic Pole.

Later Greek geographers would eventually draw maps showing imaginary horizontal lines marking boundaries between zones of hot and cold climates.

The world according to Ptolemy, showing terra incognita *at both the north and south ends of the earth*

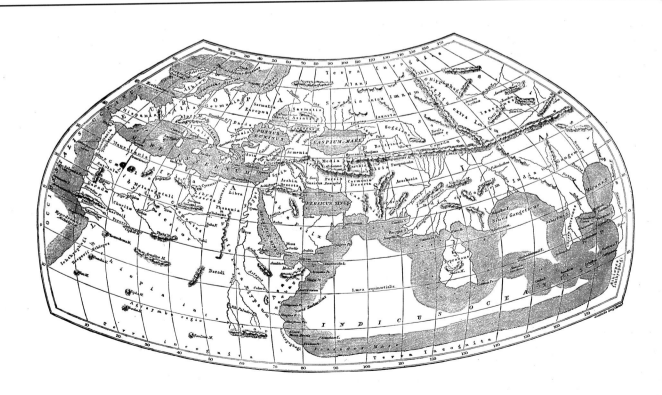

Geographer Claudius Ptolemaeus, also known as Ptolemy

They were able to define the Arctic and Antarctic circles just as they are on our maps today. No explorers had ever mapped or even seen these points, yet the Greeks were convinced that they existed. They based their belief on logical reasoning and on their knowledge of mathematics and geometry. For the Greeks, logic and science could not be wrong. Claudius Ptolemaeus, the famous geographer and astronomer of the second century A.D., even drew a map of the world with its bottom portion as a single landmass, just as we know it today. Many centuries later, explorers would prove his drawing correct, and the race for new discoveries would begin.

Science and mathematics can suggest goals for exploration; but how does one become an explorer? For Amundsen, the road toward exploration began with long ski trips in Norway. He also signed on as a crew member on Arctic seal-hunting ships.

Arctic scene

It was during his several voyages to the Arctic that Amundsen learned how to sail and survive in polar conditions. As a result of his experience, he was chosen to serve as first mate on the ship *Belgica* for its Antarctic voyage of 1897 to 1899. This would be the first expedition to stay in Antarctica for the entire winter. Prior to this, all other expeditions left before the ships became frozen into the ice. Amundsen would learn much from this first Antarctic trip, and it would benefit him years later when he would lead his own expedition to the South Pole.

After participating in the *Belgica* expedition, Amundsen acquired his own ship and began preparations for his attempt at making the first Northwest Passage. Although he would make some mistakes, he learned from them, and his expedition would develop the techniques for future polar exploration. By the time Amundsen was ready to go to the South Pole, he was probably the best trained person to do it.

The road that led Robert Falcon Scott to the South Pole was very different from Amundsen's path. Scott's knowledge of exploration was formed more from theory than from practical experience. He was also a career military man, and his character was shaped by the traditions and the way of life in Great Britain's Royal Navy. This might have made him a good naval officer, but it did not help him as an explorer. Scott looked at polar exploration as a way to get a promotion. Exploration required a decisive commander who could react well to dangerous situations. Scott decided that, as an explorer, he could be promoted to the rank of captain and command his own ship. He might even become an admiral someday, if he could succeed at some well-publicized exploration.

At the first opportunity, Scott volunteered to lead a proposed scientific expedition to Antarctica. After much discussion and deliberation, Scott was finally chosen. He would lead the British Antarctic Expedition as the commander of the ship *Discovery*.

Although the public record of the *Discovery* expedition reads very well and claimed many successes, it left some doubts. Some people felt that Scott had made several serious errors in judgment. The few who knew Antarctica well could read between the lines of Scott's report and see the real difficulties he encountered. It was apparent to them that, in many situations, Scott's decisions were no more than lucky guesses, not sound judgments. Saddest of all was the fact that Scott did not learn from his experiences and would make the same mistakes in 1911. This time he would not be so lucky, and it would cost him his life.

Chapter 2
The Early Years
of Roald Amundsen

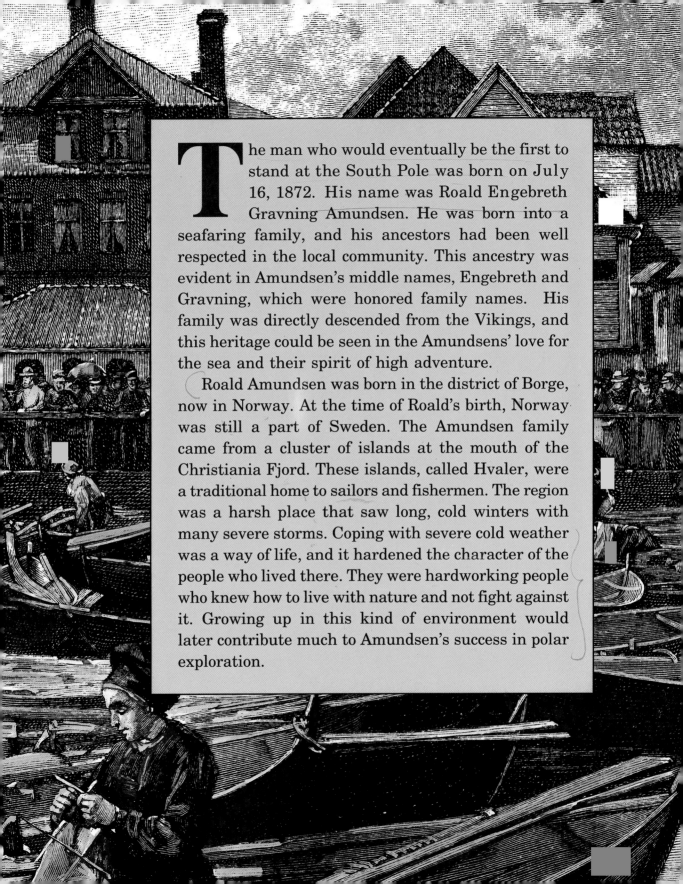

The man who would eventually be the first to stand at the South Pole was born on July 16, 1872. His name was Roald Engebreth Gravning Amundsen. He was born into a seafaring family, and his ancestors had been well respected in the local community. This ancestry was evident in Amundsen's middle names, Engebreth and Gravning, which were honored family names. His family was directly descended from the Vikings, and this heritage could be seen in the Amundsens' love for the sea and their spirit of high adventure.

Roald Amundsen was born in the district of Borge, now in Norway. At the time of Roald's birth, Norway was still a part of Sweden. The Amundsen family came from a cluster of islands at the mouth of the Christiania Fjord. These islands, called Hvaler, were a traditional home to sailors and fishermen. The region was a harsh place that saw long, cold winters with many severe storms. Coping with severe cold weather was a way of life, and it hardened the character of the people who lived there. They were hardworking people who knew how to live with nature and not fight against it. Growing up in this kind of environment would later contribute much to Amundsen's success in polar exploration.

Roald Amundsen's love for the sea was deeply rooted. His grandfather, Ole Amundsen, had five sons, and all went to sea. They all became ship captains and shipowners and very wealthy men. The fourth son was Jens Engebreth Amundsen, Roald's father. He became a ship's captain in 1853 and made a large fortune fighting the Russians in the Crimean War. In 1863, he married Hanna Henrikke Gustava Sahlquist, and they made their home in Hvidsten. This was a property near the important seaport of Sarpsborg. It was here that three of their four sons would be born. The first son, Jens Ole Antonio, was born in China during one of the voyages that Jens and Gustava took together. The Amundsen family remained at Hvidsten until three months after Roald's birth. Their next home would be in Christiania, which is now Oslo. Although they lived in the city, their property was on the edge of town. The wilds of Norway lay at their back door, and the rugged nature of the country would mold Roald's character. He grew up with a love and respect for nature firmly implanted in his heart.

The Amundsens moved to Christiania mainly because Roald's mother, Gustava, was unhappy in Hvidsten. She was very lonely there. As the daughter of a government tax official, she was accustomed to a fuller social life than Hvidsten could offer. She was also growing tired of being a ship captain's wife and raising the children alone. Jens was at sea for long periods of time during most of their marriage, and she did not like being left alone.

Life at home became more enjoyable for Gustava after moving to Christiania. There she had a household staff to supervise, and her family was near. The many activities of the capital city also helped keep her amused when Jens was away. Meanwhile, Jens continued to spend a great deal of time at sea. When he was at home, he ran the family as he did his ship. Strict discipline and obedience were the rule, and his word was law. As a ship's captain, Jens was highly respected in the community, and his sons looked up to him as more than just a father. His all-powerful image made a deep impression on Roald's young mind.

Roald's attitude toward his mother was very different. Gustava tried to balance her husband's discipline by acting more like a friend to her sons than a mother. She often behaved like an older sister and easily gave in to their demands. However, her unhappiness with her marriage occupied her feelings much of the time, and she developed no real closeness with the boys. This especially affected Roald. Because Gustava did not provide him with the affection he needed, Roald turned to his Aunt Olava and his nursemaid Betty for affection. In later years, he would remember his nursemaid more fondly than he remembered his own mother.

The early years of Roald Amundsen's life were full of outdoor activities. As the youngest in his group of childhood friends, he was often teased and bullied. Because of this, he learned early in life to stand up for himself and to fight when necessary. Roald enjoyed playing in the forest around his home. He also participated in sports and became very competitive. He and his brothers taught themselves gymnastics and skiing. Roald loved winter sports, but he enjoyed skiing the most. Skiing was the national sport of Norway, and most children learned to ski at an early age. Roald learned cross-country and downhill skiing and even became good at ski jumping.

During the school holidays, Roald and his brothers would go back to Hvidsten to enjoy country life by the sea. They learned how to handle small boats by playing at hide-and-seek among the ships at anchor. In the winter when the sea ice hardened enough, the boys would skate out for miles between the islands. But life was not always play. They also went into the shipyards to learn about building and repairing wooden-hulled ships. These experiences laid the foundation of a polar explorer. What Roald learned here as a boy would serve him well years later as he pushed back the frontiers of exploration.

Roald's academic education went hand-in-hand with his practical sea training. His father was a firm believer in the value of a good education. In Norwegian society, academic achievement was one way of attaining a higher social status. This was very important to Jens Amundsen, and he wanted his sons to further their education as much as possible. Jens had only an elementary school education when he went off to sea, and he always regretted that he did not go farther in school. At the time of his death in 1886, only one son had graduated from secondary school. Two of the other boys went off to sea as their father had, without finishing their education. Only Roald was left in school. He was fourteen at the time. His mother held high hopes that he would someday become a medical doctor, but it was not meant to be.

During his secondary school days, Roald came across the works of polar explorer Sir John Franklin. His descriptions and accounts of the Arctic region filled Roald's imagination with thoughts of exploration and made a lasting impression upon him. The Franklin expedition had ended in disaster, as all the

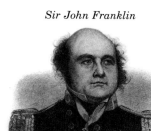

Sir John Franklin

men were eventually lost. Later rescue expeditions found no trace of them. This heroic tale of adventure excited young Amundsen, and he decided to follow in Franklin's footsteps and become a polar explorer. Roald began preparing to achieve that goal very soon. He was a very determined young man, and he knew that success began with hard work and good preparation.

Burial of a crewman from the Franklin expedition

Sir John Franklin's writings introduced Roald to polar exploration, but the accomplishments of a fellow Norwegian inspired him. In the summer of 1888, Fridtjof Nansen made the first crossing of the Greenland ice cap. This is a permanent sheet of ice that covers most of Greenland's landmass.

To make the crossing, Nansen followed an entirely new approach to polar exploration. First, he chose a route that would take him from east to west, with no provisions left over for a return along the same route. This was a bold move. It meant that he had to go forward or perish. Equally bold was Nansen's introduction of new polar equipment. For the first time, he would haul equipment on a platform that was mounted on skis.

His team also used skis to cross the ice and snow. Nansen paid very close attention to every detail. He designed a new type of cooking pan to conserve heat and fuel, and he redesigned the clothing to be worn. His expedition was the first to use a specially prepared diet for the men so they could perform to their maximum efficiency. After all, problems with food had plagued the Franklin expedition. Lead poisoning from canned food may have caused all the men to perish. Nansen did not want to repeat such a disaster, nor did he want his men so weak that they could not accomplish their goal.

The descriptions that Amundsen read of Nansen's crossing of Greenland truly inspired him. He was so taken by the excitement of the event that he and three of his friends planned their own little ski expedition. They chose a location close to Christiania that was known as Nordmarka. Their trip lasted only twenty hours, but they crossed over 50 miles (80 kilometers) of difficult country without the benefit of modern ski equipment. The skis they used and the provisions they brought were inadequate, and they were lucky to get back alive. At the end of their trip they were exhausted but exhilarated by the experience. This was only the first such trip Amundsen would make, and it did much to prepare him for what was to come.

In his schoolwork, Roald was a less-than-average student with little or no potential for university studies. He just barely managed to pass his final examinations in secondary school and receive his graduation certificate. Although he did not want to continue his education, Roald did enter the medical school at Christiania University, as his mother wished. But a career in medicine was never in Amundsen's plan, and he did not perform well in his studies. In the end, he failed his university examinations and, after his mother's death in 1893, he left school.

Roald's time at the university seemed to him only a temporary stage in his life. Now he could pursue his real ambition: to become an explorer. While Amundsen was at the university, Norway began to develop its drive for independence from Sweden. Intense feelings of nationalism swept the country, and heroes were in short supply. One hero, however, was Fridtjof Nansen, who brought international recognition to Norway through his exploration of Greenland.

Another hero was Ervind Astrup, also a polar explorer. He had accompanied the American explorer Robert Peary on a south-to-north trip across Greenland. Amundsen knew of Astrup's achievements and eagerly attended one of his lectures at the university. Roald was very impressed by Astrup's description of the conditions he encountered. Astrup emphasized the importance of learning Eskimo ways in order to be a successful Arctic explorer. European ways would not help in the Arctic, Astrup said, and one had to think like an Eskimo to survive. Amundsen took this to heart and would not forget that lesson.

Robert Peary

Fridtjof Nansen

The lure of Arctic exploration was sweeping across Norway as more and more people became aware of Nansen's and Astrup's explorations. Since Nansen was a national hero, his influence with government grew. He was able to convince the government to finance an Arctic expedition that would take a ship through the Arctic Ocean and gather scientific information along the way. The idea was simple enough: just let a ship become frozen into the ice and drift along until it reached ice-free water. According to Nansen's plan, ocean currents would carry the ship across the North Pole. He would thus become the first explorer to reach the pole. Nansen had a special ship built for this voyage. The *Fram* was designed to with-

Fjords, or cliffs along the water, in the Arctic region of Norway

stand the crushing pressure of the enclosing ice. It was a wonderful research vessel, though Nansen's plan to drift to the North Pole was not a success.

As Roald Amundsen watched the *Fram* sail from Christiania on midsummer's day, 1893, he was very envious. He wished that he could be on board heading into unknown polar regions. Roald was so taken by the excitement that he wrote to two other polar explorers and asked if they would take him on their expeditions. He was politely refused for lack of experience, but he did not give up hope of someday going on an expedition. Little did he know, on that summer's day in 1893, that he would one day be the captain of the *Fram* and take it to Antarctica.

Chapter 3
Amundsen's Long
Road to Exploration

Roald Amundsen was not a man who waited for opportunity to come knocking at his door. He preferred to take control of his own fate. Once he set his mind on a goal, he would do everything possible to achieve it. Amundsen knew that the path to polar exploration lay in gaining experience and learning from others. He also knew that his skills in skiing and seamanship were lacking, so he developed a plan to get more experience. Up to this time, Roald had only skied on the lowlands of Nordmarka, and he needed mountain experience as well. In 1893, Roald asked the expert skier Laurentius Urdahl to take him along on one of his trips to the mountains west of Oslo. The place chosen for the skiing excursion was a plateau called Hardangervidda. In winter, the conditions there were very similar to those Amundsen would later encounter in Antarctica.

This was the second time Urdahl had attempted to cross Hardangervidda. The first time, blizzards had defeated him. This time would be different, he thought. But weather conditions during this second attempt proved no better than the first, and it soon became apparent that the trip would not be a success. Delay followed delay, and the skiers found they were making no progress. Once again, Urdahl gave up and returned to Christiania.

Amundsen, however, did not give in so easily. He and another man made one final attempt to cross the plateau, but a night at -40 degrees Fahrenheit (-40 degrees Celsius) forced them to return as well. Frigid climate conditions had beaten Amundsen, but he would try again.

Six weeks later, Amundsen found himself sailing off to the Arctic Ocean. Realizing that he needed sailing as well as skiing experience, he had signed on to the sealing ship *Magdalena*. This voyage would teach him the techniques of sailing in icy waters. It would be a hard lesson in sailing, but it gave Amundsen valuable experience and he learned well.

Roald enjoyed his life aboard ship, and he found the Arctic a fascinating place. The one bad experience he had was watching the slaughter of the seals. He realized that sealing required killing the animals, but the cruel slaughter he witnessed was beyond his imagination. After this experience, Amundsen held a new respect for animal life. He knew that killing animals was necessary to obtain food and clothing, but the inhumane slaughter of so many seals did not seem right. In future years, Amundsen did kill animals for food when necessary, but he killed only as many as could be used.

Seal hunting in the Arctic

A major part of Amundsen's plan for becoming a polar explorer was to earn a master's certificate in seamanship. First he had to earn a mate's certificate, so he needed to spend as much time as possible at sea. Roald signed on to one of his family's merchant ships, but his experience there could not compare to his voyage to the Arctic. Roald longed for another chance to head north, but for now he had to remain on the merchant ship. In May 1895, Amundsen received his mate's certification, but with a disappointing second-class rating. Once again, taking examinations was very hard for Roald, but he learned seamanship well.

Time at sea on a merchant ship did nothing to discourage Amundsen from his goal of polar exploration. It was just part of his long-term plan, and he was making progress. Military service briefly interrupted his sea duty, but he used it to condition his body and mind. After his military service ended, Amundsen decided once again to attempt to cross Hardangervidda, this time with his brother Leon. The defeat it had dealt him two years before was still fresh in his mind. Roald did not take defeat lightly; he wanted to succeed this time.

Winter skiing expeditions in Norway are always dangerous. The explorer Ervind Astrup had died on a skiing trip into Norway's Rondane Mountains, but Amundsen was determined not to let that happen to him. Their trip was expected to last one week, and when there was no word of them after three weeks, they were given up for lost. Once again, weather conditions and inadequate provisions had almost finished them. Frostbitten and half-starved, they finally gave up. The brothers came home beaten but alive. Amundsen never conquered Hardangervidda, but it taught him many valuable lessons. This time, he resolved never to be so poorly prepared for an expedition again.

Shortly after the ill-fated ski trip to Hardangervidda, word came that a Norwegian whaler, the *Antarctic*, had reached the Ross Sea off Antarctica's Pacific coast. Among those who went ashore was Carsten Borchgrevink, an old childhood friend of Amundsen's. Carsten brought back wonderful news of the exploration. A British geographical society was meeting in London at the time, and news of the *Antarctic* expedition excited its members. They declared that Antarc-

Carsten Borchgrevink

tica would be a priority for British exploration, and that an expedition would be underway before the turn of the century.

Explorers of other nations considered this a challenge, and Belgium was one of the first countries to respond. A Belgian naval officer, Adrien De Gerlache, began to organize an Antarctic expedition. His choice of ship was an old Norwegian sealer, and he took it to Norway to refit it for extended polar duty. While De Gerlache's ship, newly renamed *Belgica*, was in port, Amundsen was just returning from a second polar voyage. Upon hearing news of the *Belgica* expedition, Amundsen immediately volunteered for the voyage.

The Belgica *in port*

At the time he applied for the *Belgica* expedition, Amundsen was unknown as an explorer. His background as a skier and sailor made him an excellent choice for the expedition, though, and he was accepted as first mate. For his part in the expedition, Amundsen accepted no pay. In addition, he promised to take refresher courses in navigation and to learn to speak Flemish, one of the languages of Belgium.

Belgica sailed from Ostend, Belgium, on August 23, 1897, headed for Antarctica by way of South America. The last member of the crew to join the ship was Dr. Frederick A. Cook, an American and an accomplished polar explorer. Amundsen would learn much from him as they experienced the Antarctic together.

The voyage from Belgium to Antarctica was routine up to the point where they had to pass by Cape Horn, at the tip of South America. The seas here are among the roughest in the world. During a storm off Cape Horn, a Norwegian sailor was washed overboard and drowned while Amundsen was on duty. Amundsen felt responsible for his death, even though there was nothing he could have done to prevent it. His grief over the loss of the sailor was deep, but the sight of the ice-covered continent ahead sent his spirits soaring. Antarctica was unlike any other place he had ever seen, and he was extremely grateful to be there and to see its wonders.

The primary purpose of the *Belgica* expedition was scientific, and several landings were made to obtain geological specimens and to survey the land. During one of these landings, Amundsen tried out his skis, becoming the first person to ski on the Antarctic continent. He was also a part of the first sledging party. (Sledges are sled-like vehicles used to haul supplies

over ice and snow.) As the men moved from campsite to campsite, they man-hauled (pulled) their sledges along over the ice and up over high ground. Amundsen quickly learned that this was not an efficient way to travel in Antarctica, and that a better method had to be found. This was a lesson he would not forget.

As the end of Antarctic summer neared, the expedition was far behind schedule. It seemed that De Gerlache's original plan, to make a brief exploration of the coastal area, would fail. The onset of winter had taken him by surprise. He decided to take the *Belgica* as far south as possible and let it freeze into the pack ice. By doing this, De Gerlache believed he could drift across the South Pole, the same way Nansen had tried to drift across the North Pole years before.

Explorer Frederick A. Cook in the Arctic region

33

The Antarctic winter came as a shock for most of the *Belgica* crew. No one had ever experienced an Antarctic winter before. That close to the pole, the sun was out of sight for weeks on end. The long period without sunlight played on the men's minds. Fear was a daily part of their lives. No one really knew if they would ever return home. In addition, they did not have enough food and warm clothing. Scurvy, a disease caused by lack of vitamin C, set in early. This, combined with the onset of madness, presented a serious situation for the *Belgica* crew. Their chances of surviving the winter were very poor.

It was Dr. Cook who saved the expedition. He ordered that seals be killed and eaten partially cooked. This gave the men the maximum amount of vitamin C from the seal meat. The sealskins were then used to make warm clothing. De Gerlache disagreed with Dr. Cook's methods. He ordered that seal meat be fed only to those men who asked for it. Amundsen was one of those who ate the seal meat, and his condition improved. Meanwhile, those who did not eat it began to die. It was only when the entire crew was close to death that De Gerlache agreed to let everyone eat seal meat, and all became healthy again.

The return of the sun brought back hopes of escaping the ice and returning home safely. But the ice did not break up, and they found themselves hopelessly drifting over the sea encased in ice. The thought of facing a second winter locked into the ice was unbearable. Once again, Dr. Cook came to the rescue.

Dr. Cook suggested that the crew cut a narrow canal through the ice to a small channel of water that lay in front of them. He hoped that, the next time the ice moved, it would crack and give them an escape

route. Eventually, the men sawed and blasted a canal, only to see the drifting ice close the gap again. But by a stroke of luck, the canal reopened and permitted the ship to slide free into open water. It was another month before they worked completely free and headed home. They had been trapped in the ice for thirteen months. In the end, most of the crew left the ship at the first port-of-call, and the expedition ended badly. Yet, it was not a complete failure. Its scientists had collected over a year's worth of weather data and many geological specimens. As for Amundsen, the voyage was the greatest experience of his life.

Penguins sliding on their bellies in the Antarctic

Amundsen's return from Antarctica was quiet and without celebration. He realized that the voyage was not the success they had all hoped for, but he learned much from his experiences aboard the *Belgica*. Now he was on to the next step in his plans. He would return to sea and put in enough time to qualify for his master's certificate. Once again he would serve on one of the family's merchant ships. During these long voyages, Roald read about other polar explorations in his spare time. By April 1900, Amundsen had completed his sea training and gained his master's certificate. He was now ready to lead his own expedition.

Since he was a boy, Amundsen had been excited by the search for the Northwest Passage, a sea route through the Arctic region from the Atlantic to the Pacific Ocean. The account of Sir John Franklin's expedition had been one of Amundsen's earliest inspirations. Franklin's quest for the passage had ended in disaster, however; after the crew left England in 1845, they were never seen again. A search party led by Sir Robert McClure eventually completed the passage, although they traveled part of the way on land. Amundsen hoped to prove that the Northwest Passage could be made entirely by sea. To get financial support for his voyage, however, Amundsen needed scientific goals. Therefore, he would make the North Pole region his first destination.

One of the significant findings of the *Belgica* expedition had been the position of the south magnetic pole. The true South Pole, or south geographic pole, is the point where the earth's lines of longitude meet. Magnetic compasses, however, are drawn to a different spot, over 1,500 miles (2,414 kilometers) away. We now know that this point, called the south mag-

Sir James Clark Ross locates the north magnetic pole, June 1, 1831.

netic pole, may shift as much as 5 miles (8 kilometers) in a year. The north magnetic pole follows the same pattern.

Sir James Clark Ross had reached the north magnetic pole in 1831. But measurements of the south magnetic pole seemed to suggest that the north magnetic pole may have moved since Ross was there. This created an interesting controversy, and Amundsen hoped to find the solution. He suggested that he lead an expedition to the north magnetic pole and see if it actually had moved. It would be an important scientific discovery if he succeeded.

Amundsen was an explorer and not a scientist, but he was willing to do whatever it took to make his expedition a success. He traveled to Hamburg, Germany, to learn about magnetism from the respected authority Professor Georg Newmayer. Newmayer trained Amundsen extensively in the methods of taking magnetic measurements and interpreting that information. Although Amundsen became very good at his work, he still felt unsure of his abilities. He felt that there was always more to be done before leaving on an expedition.

Next, Amundsen acquired a ship for the expedition, a twenty-nine-year-old wooden sloop named the *Gjoa*. He was proud of his ship and placed a great deal of trust in its ability to cope with Arctic conditions. In part, the *Gjoa* would attempt to drift across the north geographic pole, as Nansen had tried to do in the *Fram*. A second aspect of the expedition would be a sledging trip that would locate and measure the north magnetic pole. To accomplish this, Amundsen planned to live and travel like the Eskimos did.

Sea trials were next, and Amundsen took the *Gjoa* out in September 1901 for a five-month cruise. This would test the ship under the icy conditions he expected to encounter on the long expedition. During this cruise, the crew members would also hunt seals to raise money to pay for the ship.

Although the cruise was a financial success, the *Gjoa* was found to have some major faults. Sails alone were not enough to get the ship through the dangerous ice, and its hull had to be strengthened to resist pressure from the enclosing ice. The ship had to be totally refitted, and a motor was installed to provide enough power to navigate through the ice.

Other aspects of the expedition also caused Amundsen great concern. Two of these were the food supply and the means for traveling across the ice. Good food was an absolute necessity to keep the crew's spirits high on such a long voyage, so Amundsen hired an excellent cook. Amundsen also remembered the lessons learned from Dr. Frederick Cook on the *Belgica* expedition. For the long sledging trips across the ice, Amundsen would rely on pemmican. This food, developed by the North American Indians, was a mixture of lean ground dried meat and melted fat. It was highly nutritious, and the men could still eat fresh meat when it was available.

The Gjoa, *the vessel in which Amundsen successfully navigated the Northwest Passage*

As for transportation, Amundsen would rely on skis and on sledges pulled by dogs. The dogs chosen were Eskimo breeds from Greenland, and they proved to be valuable companions as well as hardy work animals. To use dogs successfully, Amundsen had to learn dog-driving, a difficult skill, and it took a great deal of practice before he became good at it.

The last step in his preparation was the selection of a crew. His crew would be small, only six men. Each member would be hand-picked for his special skills. Each man had his responsibilities, and Amundsen depended on each one doing his job well. Although Amundsen was clearly the captain and always in command, he shared in all the work and frequently sought the advice of the other crew members. This approach led to a friendly environment aboard the ship, and disagreements were few.

On June 16, 1903, with all preparations made, Amundsen and the *Gjoa* left Christiania for the Arctic. Amundsen's dream of leading a polar expedition had come true, and it was now up to him to make it a success. The long voyage ahead would be difficult, but the years of training and the experience he had gained would pay off.

The *Gjoa* expedition would take over three years to complete. As they threaded their way through the islands of the Canadian Arctic, they passed the last known encampment of Sir John Franklin's expedition. Amundsen treated this place as sacred ground, and he had his crew place a memorial there to the men of that lost expedition.

The Northwest Passage was not an easy voyage, and the crew often faced dangerous ice and stormy weather. Twice the ship ran aground and was almost

lost. Finding a safe harbor on King William Island, the party made camp. They named the spot Gjoa Haven and built shelters there in September. This would be their base camp for the next two years.

Left to right: Roald Amundsen, Helmer Hanssen, and Peder Ristvedt on the Gjoa *expedition*

On October 3, the *Gjoa* became frozen into the ice. From that point on, the ship was carried along by the drift of the pack ice. During that time the crew hunted caribou for food and practiced their dog-handling skills. They were often visited by Eskimos and became very friendly with them. Both the crew and the Eskimos learned from each other, and they enjoyed the visits. It was a wonderful opportunity for Amundsen to learn more about the Eskimo way of survival, and he would benefit from all he learned.

Roald Amundsen, 1906

Amundsen's first attempt to reach the north magnetic pole was not successful. The crew headed out too close to the Arctic's stormy season and ran into such severe weather that it threatened their lives. They had to turn back. Amundsen learned two quick lessons on this attempt: first, the importance making an expedition in the proper season; and second, that dog-hauling, not man-hauling, was the best means of transport. These lessons would make the difference between success and failure for him later in the Antarctic. Perhaps the most important lesson that Amundsen learned from this attempt was never to push his men or dogs beyond what they could bear.

Amundsen tried twice again to reach the magnetic pole. On the third attempt, he and Peder Ristvedt finally reached the point described by Ross in 1831 as the north magnetic pole, but it was no longer there. It was true, it had moved. Now they had to search for the new position, but luck was not with them. A broken instrument caused them to miss the actual point by 30 miles (48 kilometers). But finding the exact point was not that important, since they *did* prove that the magnetic pole had moved. The expedition made many other important scientific achievements. It mapped over 150 miles (241 kilometers) of unexplored coastline and developed new techniques that became the standard for future polar expeditions.

The *Gjoa* navigated new waterways through the Arctic and completed its passage into ice-free water. It was a successful voyage in every respect. The success of an expedition, however, is ultimately achieved when its discoveries are made public. For Amundsen, that meant that he would have to send a telegraph message announcing the successful completion of his

voyage. But by now, the *Gjoa* was once again frozen into the Arctic ice. To send a telegram, Amundsen would have to make a 500-mile (805-kilometer) ski trip from his icebound ship to Eagle City, Alaska. This was a heroic feat in itself.

The telegram was to be sent to Fridtjof Nansen, who was then to announce it to the world. But the news leaked out, and the announcement first appeared in a Seattle, Washington, newspaper. This early release of the news caused Amundsen great embarrassment. It also created an international incident between the United States and Norway, since it was a United States Army officer who leaked the news. Nevertheless, Amundsen and his crew returned to Norway as heroes. At last, Amundsen had fulfilled his dream of completing a major exploration. Little did he know that his greatest feat was yet to come.

Amundsen and crewman Hanssen in Alaska after their expedition

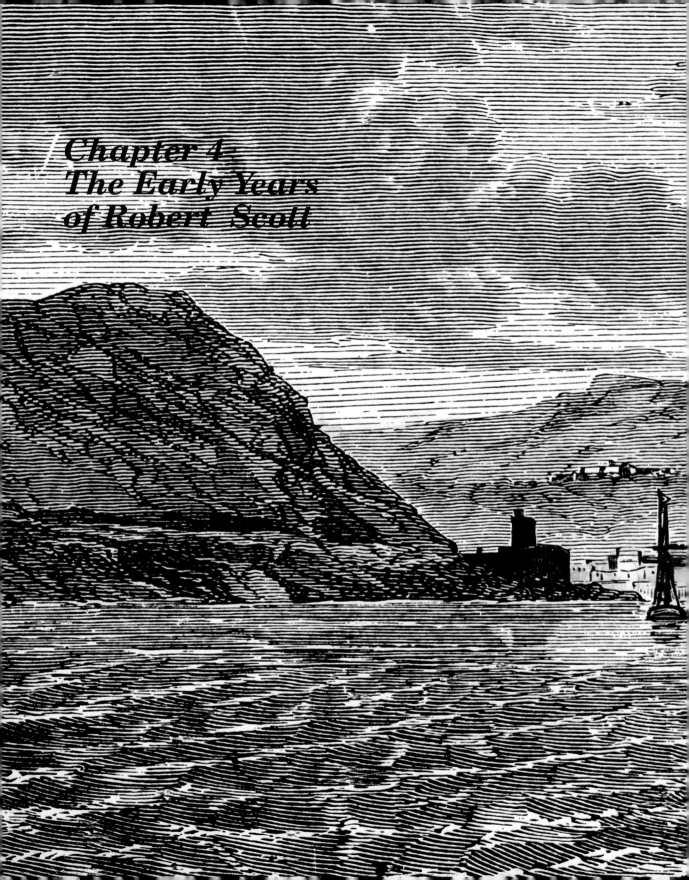

Chapter 4:
The Early Years
of Robert Scott

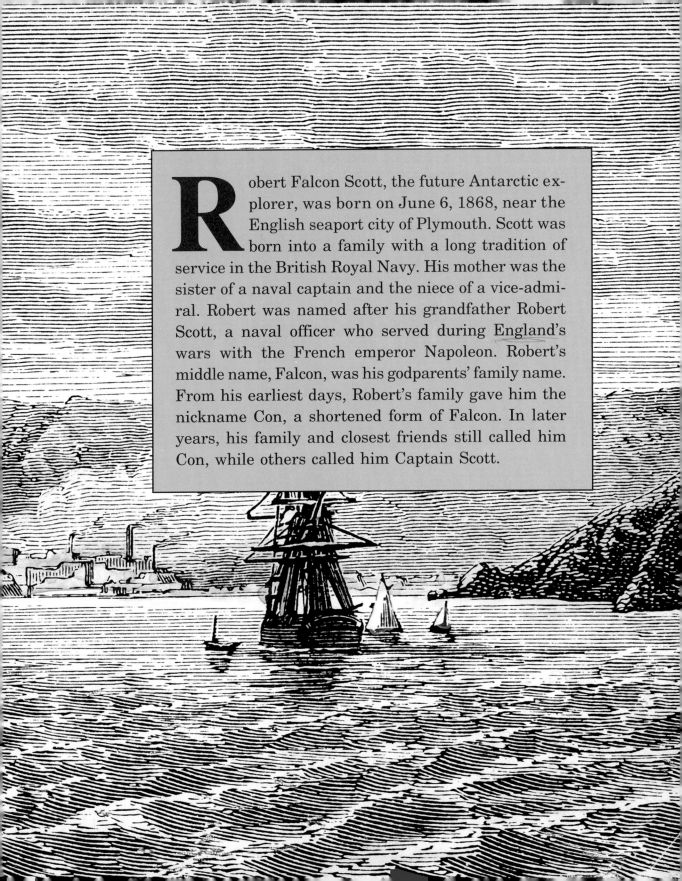

obert Falcon Scott, the future Antarctic explorer, was born on June 6, 1868, near the English seaport city of Plymouth. Scott was born into a family with a long tradition of service in the British Royal Navy. His mother was the sister of a naval captain and the niece of a vice-admiral. Robert was named after his grandfather Robert Scott, a naval officer who served during England's wars with the French emperor Napoleon. Robert's middle name, Falcon, was his godparents' family name. From his earliest days, Robert's family gave him the nickname Con, a shortened form of Falcon. In later years, his family and closest friends still called him Con, while others called him Captain Scott.

The Scott family estate where young Robert was raised, called Outlands, was in Devonport. This was also the location of Plymouth's naval dockyard. Although the family was not considered wealthy, they were financially secure. Scott's grandfather Robert had made the family fortune. He built up his wealth from his salary as a naval officer and from his share of the prize money his ship won during the Napoleonic Wars. He and his brother then purchased the Outlands property and a small brewery. The business proved successful, and Robert Scott eventually bought out his brother's share and became the sole owner of the business. This he would eventually pass on to his son John Edward, Robert Falcon Scott's father.

The older Robert Scott had four sons. Three of them joined the British army and served in India, while the youngest, John Edward, was left at home to run the family business. Of the four brothers, John was the least suited to the task. He was a quiet and depressed man who did not think well of himself. John felt unfit to run the family business, and he often had violent fits of temper. Perhaps it was because he was the youngest of the boys. He always tried to be as good as his older brothers, but he felt that he did not measure up to the standards they set. When his father died, John Edward inherited the Outlands estate and the brewery. He eventually sold the business and lived off the money from the sale.

John Edward Scott enjoyed the life of a country gentlemen, and he spent a good deal of time gardening. Outwardly he appeared to be a happy man, but he was not emotionally strong, and his weakness of character often showed through. Unfortunately, young Robert would inherit many of his father's traits.

The Scott household at Outlands was very large. John Edward and Hannah Scott had six children, four girls and two boys. In addition, there were nine servants and a relative living with them. Although John gave the appearance of authority, it was Hannah who really ran the household. She managed her servants very well, and kept a home appropriate to their lifestyle. Hannah had a stronger spirit than her husband, and her wishes were law. Although she expressed concern for others, she was strong-minded and always did things her way. For better or worse, her attitude and her way of life influenced Robert long after she was gone.

The bustling, commercial port city of Plymouth, near Robert Falcon Scott's birthplace

47

Romanticized picture of a young boy working on board a ship

As a boy, Robert led a rather sheltered life. He was not an especially healthy child, but he was a likable little boy. In most respects, he was like other upper-middle-class children of his time. He began his education at home under a governess, and at the age of eight he went to school with the other children. There he continued his education until he was thirteen. Robert's education and his future career were decided by his father. The child was given no choice. For Robert and his younger brother Archibald, their father chose a military career. Robert would prepare for a career in the Royal Navy, and Archibald would serve in the army. They did as they were told.

Sailors "manning the yards" for a naval review by the queen

To enter into the Royal Navy for officer's training, Robert first had to pass an entrance examination. His father took him out of school and sent him to a special tutoring program designed to prepare students for the naval entrance exams. Robert did well in his studies and passed the examination. At the age of thirteen, he became a naval cadet and was assigned to the training ship *Britannia*. Here he would learn the traditions and way of life of the Royal Navy. As a cadet, Robert learned the navy's "spit-and-polish" style of discipline. The navy also taught him to obey authority blindly, without questioning it. What it did not teach him was how to think independently.

Scott's naval education began at Dartmouth, a school much like other private schools in England at the time. In many ways the school had a repressive climate. At Dartmouth, Robert studied the subjects required to function as a good naval officer. Cadet Scott would learn navigation, mathematics, and seamanship, although he did not study the proper use of the English language. It was not considered necessary for a good officer to express himself correctly. He was to learn what was needed and no more. This flaw in the educational system forced many students into a very narrow way of thinking.

A second flaw in Scott's naval education was that promotion in rank was based on academic achievements alone. A person's leadership ability was not considered in the promotion process. In his studies, Scott did well. He graduated seventh in his class of twenty-six and was rated a midshipman. Yet, no one knew whether or not Scott possessed an ability to command. That, it seems, was not important for an officer of that time.

Following his studies at Dartmouth, Scott spent four years at sea getting practical experience. After his sea duty, he was automatically promoted to sublieutenant and sent on for further study at the Royal Naval College in Greenwich. Here Scott did extremely well, finishing very near the top of his class. He achieved four first-class certificates out of a possible five. This qualified him for further promotions, but additional sea duty had to follow first.

After completing his studies at the Royal Naval College, Scott was assigned to the cruiser HMS *Amphion*, with a temporary transfer to the HMS *Caroline*. Promotion to the rank of lieutenant came on

August 16, 1889. He had just turned twenty-one, and his naval career was progressing well. At this point in Scott's life, there was not even a hint that he would become an explorer the world would remember. Scott's major concern was simply being a good officer and doing his duty.

Lieutenant Scott returned to the *Amphion* in March 1890 and followed a normal peacetime tour of duty. Life aboard the *Amphion* became rather routine even for a new officer, and Scott looked for new ways to achieve promotion. He felt that the best way to do this was to learn about the new technology that was coming into the navy. Scott chose to study torpedoes and entered the training school at Portsmouth. In August 1893, he received his first-class certificate and qualified as torpedo lieutenant, but it was not without some difficulty. Just before completion of his training, Scott was given temporary command of a torpedo boat. During a training exercise, he ran the boat aground and was severely reprimanded for the error. Scott's first command was a big disappointment, and it clearly showed that he was better with theory than with actual situations.

Once again, Lieutenant Scott settled into the routine of naval life. He did his job well, but it appears that he went unnoticed where promotions were concerned. Life at home was not as calm. His father had depleted the family fortune, and the Scotts were having serious financial problems. The family home of Outlands had to be rented out, and his father went to work as a brewery manager. Two of his sisters left home at this time, and his brother in the army was transferred from India to a less-desirable post in Nigeria. Times were not good for the Scott family.

In 1897, Scott's father died, and one year later his brother Archibald died of typhoid fever. His mother and two sisters then moved to London, with the two girls taking up dressmaking to support themselves. The one bright spot for Scott was that his sister Ettie had married a man who had influence with the Admiralty. This was the office that ruled over British naval affairs. Scott hoped this new connection would improve his chances of getting promoted. He knew that having influence in the right places was the key to success. Now Scott truly believed his time had come.

Promotion in rank was the mark of a successful military career, but promotions were hard to come by during peacetime conditions. In war, special heroism leads to a quick promotion, but during peacetime, one had to seek out other means for recognition. Outstanding officers are always noticed, and they can eventually be promoted to captain of a battleship or even admiral of a fleet. Scott hoped to achieve these goals one day, although he did not particularly stand out from the other officers. Still, Scott actively sought ways to improve his chances for promotion. Knowing the "right people" and taking part in an exploration were two paths to promotion, and Scott realized that he would need both to fulfill his dreams.

Sir Francis Drake

In Scott's time, exploration had become a proud tradition of the Royal Navy. It offered Scott the opportunity he was looking for, and he would make every effort to be appointed to lead an expedition. From Sir Francis Drake to Captain James Cook, the British boasted of many successful expeditions. Exploration provided a good test of ship captains and crew, and it offered situations normally found only in war. But there were other reasons for exploring. On their voy-

Norwegian Carsten Borchgrevink's 1894 Antarctic expedition (shown here) spurred other nations to explore the icy continent

ages, explorers encountered new lands and people far different from those in England. More importantly, exploration often led to the accumulation of new riches, and later, the colonization of new lands. Financial gain was the real motive behind British exploration. In the Royal Navy, great explorers became national heroes and gained quick promotions.

By this time, the north and south poles were among the few unexplored regions in the world. The leading advocate of polar exploration in England at this time was Sir Clements Markham, the president of the Royal Geographical Society. He himself had served in the Royal Navy and participated in the second Franklin search expedition to the Arctic in 1850 to 1851. From this experience he developed a lifelong love of polar exploration. In later years, Sir Clements helped young naval officers get their chance at exploration. Robert Falcon Scott would be one of these.

Sir Clements Markham idealized the self-sacrifice and suffering that polar exploration required. He felt that heroism could not be achieved without facing death. He believed that the most difficult path provided the greatest glory. Sir Clements even believed that lasting glory could be found in defeat, if the effort was heroic and deserved admiration.

One of Sir Clements Markham's dreams was to sponsor a polar expedition that would produce heroes for the British public to admire. He began plans to organize such an expedition, but the process was very slow and it met with little support. In the meantime, the Norwegian explorer Carsten Borchgrevink proposed a voyage to Antarctica, and a London newspaper owner gave him financial support. Borchgrevink was the first to spend the winter on the continent of Antarctica, and his expedition was a great success.

The midnight sun in Antarctica, as drawn by a member of Borchgrevink's party

All this took place while Sir Clements waited anxiously for the financial support to begin his expedition. In March 1899, he finally received the money he needed to organize and equip the British Antarctic Expedition.

Next, he began to look for an expedition leader. This was perhaps the most important aspect of the expedition. Markham wanted a leader who was skilled but could also represent England in the eyes of the world. He considered youth, stamina, and personality to be far more important than experience.

After interviewing hundreds of young naval officers, two men seemed closest to what Sir Clements had in mind. It appears from his interview notes that Sir Clements's first choice was Thomas C. Smyth, a competent naval officer who came from a well respected family. He had both leadership abilities and the personality traits that Sir Clements valued. The second choice was Robert Falcon Scott.

This was not the first time Scott and Sir Clements Markham had met. Their first meeting took place after a boat race that Scott entered while he was a midshipman in 1887. Further social meetings occurred in 1890 and 1891. By this time they were acquaintances, but not yet good friends. This changed during one of Sir Clements's visits to the fleet. Scott was serving as torpedo lieutenant on the HMS *Empress of India*, and he was invited to dine with Sir Clements. Scott made a favorable impression on Sir Clements, and he would not be forgotten. They met again in June 1899, after the announcement of the British Antarctic Expedition and its plans of exploration. During an afternoon tea, Scott volunteered to lead the expedition, and he would not take no for an answer.

From 1899 to 1902, England was involved in the Boer War against descendants of Dutch settlers in South Africa.

Why did Scott want to lead the British Antarctic Expedition so badly? Up to this point in his life, he had never expressed any interest in polar exploration. The answer was quite obvious. This was his best chance to gain the promotion he so desperately sought.

As fate would have it, world political conditions began to change. Western Europe was becoming restless, and Germany began to expand its fleet for a possible challenge to Britain's powerful navy. Britain, at this time, was already involved in a war in South Africa. These events began to put pressure on the Royal Navy, and its officers became less interested in polar exploration when the possibility of war with Germany was very real. Scott, however, remained firm in his commitment to polar exploration.

The final move that would send Scott to the Antarctic was made by his leading competitor for the

A portrait of Robert Falcon Scott in his naval uniform

position, Thomas Smyth. He was Sir Clements's first choice, but he had disgraced himself because of a drinking problem. Scott now had the advantage. All he had to do now was to remain visible to the selection committee and wait for their announcement. Sir Clements urged Scott to be patient.

Word finally came that Scott had been chosen. He would be promoted to the rank of commander and would lead the expedition with Lieutenant Charles Rawson Royds as his assistant. Scott finally achieved the first step in his grand plan for advancement. As it turns out, after waiting ten years for a promotion to commander, he had already been recommended for that position. Within three or four years, the promotion would have been his, but that was too slow for Scott. He knew he had made the right decision in choosing polar exploration.

Chapter 5
The Discovery Expedition

The British Antarctic Expedition of 1901 to 1904, also called the *Discovery* expedition, would be the first scientific exploration of the Antarctic interior. Up to this time, several expeditions had mapped and surveyed a few sections of the Antarctic coastline. But most of the continent remained unexplored. Explorers who went ashore did move inland, but they never got very far from their ships and the sea. What was known of the interior was very exciting, but it only hinted at what lay beyond the horizon. It was hoped that the *Discovery* expedition would change all that.

Robert Falcon Scott received the command he so desperately sought, and the *Discovery* expedition was now his. Yet, the situation was not as good as it seemed. Scott was selected as commander not for his professional skills, but for making a good impression on Sir Clements Markham. Scott was well aware of his lack of experience in polar exploration, and he did try to remedy it. He studied the published records of earlier expeditions, and he sought the advice of Fridtjof Nansen, the greatest polar explorer of his day. Based on his own experiences, Nansen advised Scott well, but Scott would not take his advice. Scott had his own ideas, and he tended to listen only to those who supported his ideas. When he was shown to be wrong, he simply ignored the good advice.

Scott had problems with the *Discovery* expedition from the start. There was much quarreling about the selection of crew members. Scott finally selected the men who would lead the various scientific aspects of the expedition. Among them were the veteran Antarctic explorer Louis Bernacchi and the medical doctor Edward Wilson, who was also a biologist and artist. Among Scott's officers was a young man named Ernest Shackleton, the future Antarctic rival who would lead his own expedition in 1908.

As the *Discovery* left port in August 1901, it was hailed as the best-equipped scientific expedition to sail for Antarctica. Actually, the ship was badly overloaded and had developed a leaky hull. It was not the best beginning to a dangerous voyage. Nevertheless, exploration and science were its goals, and its captain and crew were determined to succeed. Scott's orders were to explore the Ross Ice Shelf, a huge sheet of ice on the Pacific Ocean side of Antarctica. Then he was

to search inland for Antarctica's high mountain range. *Antarctica's Admiralty Mountains*
He was also to make numerous scientific observations
and to conduct various experiments along the way.

On January 1, 1902, the *Discovery* reached the
Ross Sea off the coast of the Ross Ice Shelf. In the sea
floated huge chunks of ice, called pack ice. As the ship
slipped through the drifting icebergs, Scott was amazed
by both the danger and the beauty of the icebergs. At
one point, the *Discovery* was almost crushed against
the side of a giant iceberg. The tide had changed and
caught the ship, carrying it into the path of several
icebergs. It was only when the tide suddenly shifted
again that the ship was able to make for open water
and safety. This showed Scott that survival in the
Antarctic could depend on luck as much as skill. Unfortunately, he would later depend too much on luck
and disregard the skill that would insure safety.

Steep ice cliffs like this one are serious obstacles to Antarctic explorers

Edward VII of England

One of the *Discovery*'s first scientific observations proved that the Ross Ice Shelf was actually floating upon the Ross Sea. The Barrier, as the shelf was then called, proved to be a continuous expanse of ice that ranged from 70 to 240 feet (21 to 73 meters) in height. It truly proved to be a barrier to further progress inland, and Scott headed east to get around it. He named the land on the Barrier's eastern edge King Edward VII Land, in honor of the king of England.

In an attempt to see what was beyond the Barrier, Scott made the first hot-air balloon ascent over Antarctica. At first Scott was frightened, since it was his first time up in a balloon, but he overcame his fear. He saw from the balloon that the ice shelf was a continuous, wavelike expanse that extended southward toward the interior with no apparent end. It

62

seemed to him that any future expedition would first have to contend with this treacherous Barrier.

After the balloon flight, Scott next sought to establish his first winter camp. He chose to remain aboard the ship rather than to build a structure on shore. The site he selected was alongside an island on the west side of the ice shelf. It was 400 miles (644 kilometers) farther south than any previous winter camp, and Scott was proud of this achievement. He named the place Hut Point. Scott and his men would spend the winter here learning how to live and work in the Antarctic. Perhaps the most important lesson to be learned was how to handle the sled dogs. One thing Scott learned from Nansen was the importance of sled dogs on an Antarctic expedition, provided they were managed properly.

The many activities of Scott's Antarctic expedition included making scientific observations of emperor penguins (above)

63

Success did not come easily for the *Discovery* expedition. Scott's first three sledging trips proved disastrous. The first sledging party came down with scurvy and had to return quickly. Scott, in the second party, was driven back by intense cold weather and problems with his dogs. His Siberian dogs, which Nansen said were not suited for the Antarctic, were proving to be very difficult to handle. The third party was caught in a blizzard and panicked. On the way back to camp, one man was lost when he fell off an ice cliff and went into the sea. The second man just barely made it back. In his journal, Scott expressed his feelings of disappointment: ". . . each journey had been a failure; we had little or nothing to show for our labors. . . . Everything was wrong, the whole system was bad. . . ." This was definitely not the start he had expected.

The sun set on the *Discovery* expedition on April 23, 1902, and winter set in. During the long months of darkness, the men went over their mistakes and made preparations for the next season's activities. Time was also spent in keeping spirits high. Shackleton and Wilson published a newspaper called the *South Polar Times*, poetry recitals were held, and shows were put on for entertainment. But the one thing that they all waited for was the return of the sun. Its reappearance brought joy to the men, and they eagerly awaited the opportunity to get on with their exploration.

The main goal for the 1902–1903 season was to achieve a long sledge journey south, and perhaps even reach the South Pole. The journey was to be made by Scott, Wilson, and Shackleton. They would take along with them three sledges and nineteen dogs. Although they were better prepared than the previous year, trouble set in early, as the Siberian dogs found the pulling too hard. Later, several dogs became ill from eating spoiled food.

Three weeks after their journey began, the explorers faced south and looked upon land that no human eyes had ever seen. Ahead of them appeared an endless expanse of ice, broken only by occasional mountain peaks. By now, Scott realized that it would not be possible to reach the South Pole. They were running low on fuel oil and food. Some of the dogs were dying, and the men were coming down with scurvy. Yet, there was much to be done before they turned back, and they had to go forward.

Scott and his companions were 300 miles (483 kilometers) south of Hut Point by December 21, 1902. They were still on the ice shelf and had not yet reached the Antarctic mainland. By now Shackleton had come down with scurvy, and his health was a major concern. It was apparent that the canned food they brought along was not sufficient, and they turned to seal meat instead. It temporarily improved Shackleton's condition, but Scott decided that they had gone as far south as they could. They had to turn back. Still, the party had reached a new "farthest-south" point. It would do for now!

The return to Hut Point was very difficult. One by one the dogs weakened. Scott ordered that they be put out of their misery, and they were shot. This episode was very upsetting to Scott, and he swore that he would never again subject dogs to such suffering. An alternate means of transportation had to be found. Once all the dogs were gone, the men had to rely on man-hauling to pull their sledges. This was extremely hard work even for a healthy man, and in their weakened state, it was torture.

Conditions grew worse as their food supply ran low. Shackleton was the one affected most by scurvy, but he bravely pulled along. As their supply of seal meat ran out, all three began to show signs of scurvy. On February 3, 1903, the three explorers finally staggered back into Hut Point. They had been out on the Ross Ice Shelf for ninety-three days. For their efforts, they had attained a new record for the farthest south, but it almost cost them their lives.

Much had happened while Scott was on the Ross Ice Shelf. Another group on the expedition had climbed a glacier through the Transantarctic Mountains and reached the icy Polar Plateau beyond. It appeared that the Antarctic interior was a flat, high-altitude ice plateau that extended all the way to the South Pole. Once an explorer reached the plateau, the rest of the journey to the South Pole should be relatively easy. But getting to the plateau first required going over huge glaciers and crossing many dangerous crevasses, or deep cracks. There was no easy route to the pole, and those who would attempt it had to face dangers much greater than they had imagined.

The appearance of the relief ship *Morning* was a welcome sight to the weary explorers. It brought news from home and fresh supplies. Scott's ship *Discovery* was still frozen into the ice and could not leave when *Morning* sailed for home. It would remain frozen in for at least another season. Scott offered some of his men the chance to go home, and seven accepted. Joining these men was Ernest Shackleton, but it was not his choice. Scott ordered Shackleton home because of his health. Shackleton deeply resented Scott's orders, since he was fully recovered from scurvy by this time. He felt that Scott had sent him home for personal reasons and not out of concern for his health. He vowed to return to Antarctica as soon as possible to wipe out the disgrace of being sent home. From that time on, Shackleton and Scott would no longer be friends but rivals in Antarctic exploration.

Scott's second winter at Hut Point was spent restoring his strength and health. He made preparations for a new series of explorations, this time toward the west, but he would not attempt the pole again. In October 1903 he set out on the path of the previous season's party over the Transantarctic Mountains and on to the Polar Plateau.

Although scurvy was not a problem this time, the cold temperatures and high altitude of the plateau wore the party down. After sledging over 300 miles (483 kilometers), they had to give up and return. On the way back, they wandered into an ice-free valley and found a lake with running water. It was an extremely welcome sight and it renewed the men's spirits for a while.

As on Scott's earlier polar journey, lack of food and inadequate clothing were once again a problem. Because of this, Scott began to send members of the party back to camp in separate groups. Finally, only Scott, Edgar Evans, and William Lashly continued on. Toward the end of their journey they became hopelessly lost during a storm. Without warning, the party slipped on an icy slope and slid uncontrollably downhill. They landed in a snow bank that was right alongside their original trail back to Hut Point. Luck had been with them. From there, the return was easy. Scott came back to camp as the only man to have been both the farthest south and the farthest west on Antarctica. He was very proud of his achievement.

The Discovery *being towed through the icebergs of the Ross Sea*

As summer passed on, the ice that held *Discovery* did not melt, and it looked as if it would be frozen in for yet another year. Scott was extremely disappointed that they were still trapped in the ice. Then, on January 5, 1904, two relief ships, the *Morning* and the *Terra Nova*, appeared. Although he was glad to see these ships, the orders they brought were a blow to Scott. He was ordered to abandon *Discovery* and come home with them. Reluctantly, Scott began to transfer his equipment and scientific collections across the ice to the relief ships. Meanwhile, men from all three ships began to cut and blast the ice in an effort to free *Discovery*. Once again luck was on Scott's side, and the ship was released from its icy prison.

Pack ice off the Ross Ice Shelf

Discovery broke free of the ice on February 16, 1904. The expedition had been in Antarctica for over two years and two months. It had been an extremely successful scientific expedition. For the first time, the Polar Plateau had been explored, and Scott had pushed 207 miles (333 kilometers) farther south than anyone ever had before him. Perhaps the greatest benefit derived from the expedition was the experience gained from spending time in Antarctica. The explorers had learned much about polar regions simply by living there and experiencing the ever-changing conditions. Unfortunately, Scott did not learn from all his experiences and mistakes, and he would make the same mistakes seven years later.

Mount Erebus, a glacier-covered volcano on Ross Island

Public acclaim for Scott's achievements was soon to come, and he was hailed as a national hero. Yet, the Admiralty was not so positive. After all, Scott had let his ship become frozen into the ice, and it could easily have been lost. The Admiralty was greatly angered that two relief ships had to be sent to bring Scott home. The expedition's organizers were also being blamed for mismanagement and poor organization.

As Scott was returning home, he began to fear that his Antarctic achievements would not bring him the promotion he had hoped for. In part, he was right. His rapid promotion from lieutenant to commander did not set well with many older officers, and they were not supportive of Scott. When reports of Scott's disagreements with other officers and his errors in judgment came to light, many expressed doubt about Scott's ability to command. It was not the welcome home he had expected, and Scott was very disappointed by the turn of events.

Once again, Sir Clements Markham came to Scott's aid. Sir Clements had Scott's official report sent directly to King Edward VII, and the king responded by sending Scott a letter of congratulations. This letter was later printed in the newspaper, and Scott's enemies at the Admiralty would not dare to go against the king's praise. Scott's reputation was saved, and he became a hero. Finally Scott did receive his promotion, but only after the *Discovery* sailed into Portsmouth harbor on September 10, 1904. Despite all his fears, Scott had reached an important goal.

After his return from Antarctica, Scott began writing a book about his exploration. He was an excellent writer, and his book, *The Voyage of Discovery*, was a great success. It became very popular with the public, and it made the Antarctic continent real for many people who never even knew it existed. Scott became a popular lecturer and his fame grew. Yet, those who were there with him knew that he was presenting a very different picture of Antarctica than what they knew it to be. The book's account differed greatly from Scott's personal diaries. Perhaps he did not want the full truth to be known, but rather a certain point of view. On the other hand, he may not have meant to deceive. Perhaps Scott was simply good at turning dry reports of day-to-day activities into exciting reading. For whatever reason, Scott's book excited the public, and he became a national hero.

Chapter 6
The Pole at Last!

Roald Amundsen's lifelong dream was to be the first to reach the north geographic pole. His long years of preparation and his *Belgica* and *Gjoa* voyages had paved the way for success. Things were going very well for Amundsen as he was organizing his expedition. Raising the funds to cover his costs was a major worry for Amundsen. Thanks to the organizational skills of his brother Leon, and the financial help of Don Pedro Christophersen, he was able to finance the trip. The next problem was to procure a ship for the expedition. That was solved through the generosity of Fridtjof Nansen. Nansen authorized the use of his ship, the *Fram*, and Amundsen was delighted. Now all that was left was to select his crew and set sail for the Pacific Northwest.

Amundsen's ship the Fram *was formerly Nansen's ship*

Amundsen's plan was to outfit the *Fram* for a seven-year voyage. He proposed to leave Norway in early 1910 and sail around the tip of South America and then north to San Francisco, California. This was a long voyage but it could not be avoided, since the Panama Canal was not yet available for a faster passage. From San Francisco, he would go on to Point Barrow, Alaska, and then on into the polar sea. According to his plan, the *Fram* would become frozen into the ice and slowly drift across the polar region, as it had under Nansen. During this drift, Amundsen would make a dash for the North Pole. It was a good plan, and Amundsen had made every possible preparation. Success was almost assured.

As fate would have it, Amundsen would not be the first to reach the North Pole. Before he left, explorers Frederick Cook and Robert Peary both claimed to have reached the pole. A controversy immediately broke out. Regardless of the outcome, Amundsen's hope for being the first was over. All his expedition could do now was to duplicate something that had already been done twice before. This did not appeal to Amundsen, and he began to search for a new goal. Now his attention turned to the South Pole.

Ernest Shackleton, whom Scott had sent home from Antarctica, had his eye on the South Pole, too. In 1908, he led an expedition of his own to Antarctica. He reached the south magnetic pole in 1909, but failed to reach the geographic pole. However, Shackleton did set a new farthest-south record, at 97 miles (156 kilometers) from the South Pole. Meanwhile, Robert Scott was raising funds for yet another trip. He, too, hoped to be the first to reach the South Pole.

Robert Edwin Peary upon his return from the North Pole in 1909

Roald Amundsen was well aware of Scott and his plan. Now that the North Pole had been reached, Amundsen quietly began preparing for an Antarctic expedition. He would try to beat Scott to the South Pole. The trip could be made as part of his long Arctic journey. Since he had to sail around the tip of South America anyway, he could easily head for Antarctica from there. Amundsen approached the long and difficult journey to the South Pole as he would approach a typical Norwegian ski trip. He felt that, with a well-prepared, properly equipped team, the South Pole would be his for the taking.

Preparations for the voyage moved ahead, and Amundsen was able to keep his South Pole plans secret. The *Fram* set sail on June 7, 1910, Norway's Independence Day. Amundsen first took the *Fram* out into the North Atlantic for sea trials and later returned for some minor repairs. Finally, on August 9, the *Fram* headed south. Amundsen's true goal still remained a secret. Only his brother knew the truth. Even the crew did not know their real destination, and they wondered why there were so many sledge dogs on board.

The mystery was soon solved. The *Fram* stopped at the island of Madeira for some minor repairs, and as they were about to leave port, Amundsen revealed his plans to the crew. He offered every man the opportunity to return home, but they all agreed to follow him to the pole. The next thing Amundsen did was to inform Scott of his plans. By now Scott was well ahead of Amundsen, and his ship, the *Terra Nova*, was in Melbourne, Australia, when the word came. The cablegram was dated October 3, 1910, and he received it on October 13. Amundsen's message read, "Beg leave to inform you *Fram* proceeding Antarctic Amundsen." The race was now on!

On January 15, 1911, Amundsen and the crew of the *Fram* arrived at the Bay of Whales on the Ross Ice Shelf and began establishing winter quarters there. Scott was now only ten days ahead of Amundsen. His time advantage was gone, and Amundsen appeared to be in the better position. In choosing the Bay of Whales site, Amundsen was taking a risk. The Ross Ice Shelf was thought to be too dangerous a spot for building a camp. Amundsen based his choice on his experience with Arctic ice, and thereby placed himself 60 miles (97 kilometers) closer to the pole than Scott. It was an important advantage.

Sled dogs napping aboard the Fram

77

It worried Amundsen that Scott planned to follow the route toward the pole that Shackleton had already established two years before. The Norwegian gambled that he would be able to find another route through the Transantarctic Mountains and reach the Polar Plateau without too much difficulty. Amundsen was also concerned that Scott's party was so large and that they were using newly developed experimental motor sledges. Scott's expedition appeared to be far better equipped than Amundsen's, although in reality it was not. Nevertheless, Scott's activities were a major concern for Amundsen.

Amundsen named his winter headquarters Framheim. The *Fram* was anchored at the edge of the ice shelf, 2 miles (3 kilometers) away. Some of the men quickly went to work building a wooden structure that had been prepared in Norway, while others began hunting to lay in a large supply of fresh meat.

Evening at Framheim

Amundsen did not want to suffer another outbreak of scurvy like he had seen on the *Belgica* expedition. He took great care to make sure that Framheim was as secure as possible for the long winter. The wooden building was warm and comfortable, and a snow cave was carved out for use as a sauna. Life at Framheim was pleasant, and the crew spent their time preparing for the polar journey that would begin in the spring. The only excitement that broke the routine was a visit by the *Terra Nova* and members of Scott's party. The meeting was friendly but cautious. Neither crew wanted to reveal its expedition's plans. Clearly, feelings were strained between them.

Before the dark of the Antarctic winter set in, numerous supply depots had to be set up along the route toward the pole. The Norwegians realized that it would be difficult, but they knew they could handle the task. The Eskimo dog teams they had brought were working well, and the men traveled well on skis. Seven supply depots were set up along the route, with a total of 3 tons (3,048 kilograms) of food. Ample food and fuel was placed in reserve. Amundsen believed in taking calculated risks, but he was not reckless. His preparations took into account the unexpected, so that changing weather conditions would not endanger their lives. Once all the preparations were in order, they reviewed the problems they had on their sledging trips and made corrections. Many items of clothing were altered to make them better fitting or more efficient. No aspect was left unnoticed. Items such as dog harnesses and sledges were redesigned to do the job better. Everything was progressing well. All that remained was the return of the sun, and they would be off for the pole.

As the spring season began, Amundsen was anxious to get going. All through the winter he thought of Scott and wondered about his progress. An early start was absolutely necessary to get there first, and Amundsen did not want to miss the chance. Unfortunately, starting so early was a big mistake, though not one that would prove fatal.

On September 8, 1911, Amundsen gave the word to start for the pole. Weather conditions were still very cold and unpredictable, but Amundsen thought it would be all right. Once before, in the Arctic, he began a sledging trip too soon and it proved to be the wrong decision. He remembered this very well, but still chose to go ahead. The first two days went well, but then the weather changed. Conditions became unbearable and very dangerous. Amundsen knew he had made a mistake and ordered an immediate return to camp. At first it was an orderly return, but it later turned into a mad dash. The team split up, with Amundsen and two others in the lead and the remaining men strung out far behind. This was not a good move on Amundsen's part. The men left behind were in danger, and they felt that Amundsen had abandoned them. It was Hjalmar Johansen, an old, experienced polar explorer, who brought the men home and perhaps saved one man's life. Upon their return to camp, Johansen and Amundsen got into a bitter quarrel about Amundsen's actions. His authority was definitely in question, and Amundsen had to do something fast to restore his men's confidence.

One by one Amundsen approached his men and asked for a declaration of loyalty. Most of the men gave it, with the notable exception of Johansen. Johansen was a forceful man, and he could easily

Hjalmar Johansen

influence the others. Amundsen found it necessary to exclude Johansen and his followers from the journey to the pole. Instead, Johansen was assigned to lead an exploration team to King Edward VII Land, to the east of the Ross Ice Shelf. Johansen refused Amundsen's orders, and the bitterness between them grew. Later Johansen submitted to Amundsen's authority, but it was too late. Amundsen would never forgive Johansen for his disloyalty and even refused to speak to him. The feud between Amundsen and Johansen was the low point of the expedition.

One of the towering ice ridges Amundsen encountered on his trek into Antarctica's interior

The second trek toward the pole began on October 19, when Amundsen and four others set out across the Ross Ice Shelf. The team made good progress until they reached the high mountains. Here they had to follow many glaciers through the mountains, and travel became extremely rough. To move forward, both men and double dog teams had to pull the sledges. For a while it looked as if they would never get to the Polar Plateau. Blizzards added to their problems, and conditions became life-threatening. It was only their training and determination that got them through.

Once the men reached the Polar Plateau, the worst was behind them and the journey became easier. Amundsen described this part of the trip as no worse than a typical Norwegian ski trip. They made excellent progress. At 95 miles (153 kilometers) from the pole, Amundsen set up the last supply depot. Now the

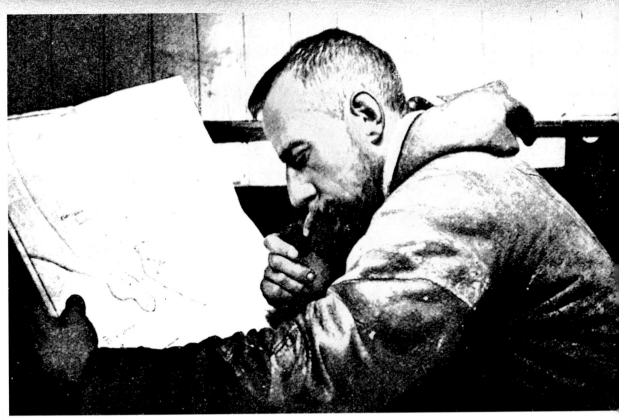
Amundsen studying his maps

sledges were lighter, and the final leg of the journey would be easier. Since they were only taking exactly what they needed to reach the pole, they marked this last depot with a long line of black poles. Their survival depended upon finding it on their return.

Reaching the pole was not the major problem as they left the last depot on December 10, but finding it was. Navigation in polar regions is very difficult, and they had to be sure that their measurements were correct. They did not want to lose the pole to Scott through errors in calculating its position. The men knew they were very close to the pole as they broke camp on December 14. They were all nervous, since they would soon find out whether Scott had beaten them. Win or lose, the men knew their journey was nearly over, and a certain sense of relief came over them. But where were the British?

As the Norwegian team approached the pole, Helmer Hanssen was leading the party. He was the best dog handler, and his usual position was out in front. But Hanssen had no wish to be the first man at the South Pole; that honor belonged to Amundsen. Judging that the pole was very near, Hanssen called on Amundsen to take the lead. Amundsen took the lead at 3:00 P.M., skiing furiously ahead while the rest of the party fell behind. Soon the others stopped and shouted, "Halt!" Amundsen had already reached the pole, and he didn't even know it, but his men made sure that he got the glory he deserved.

The four men who reached the South Pole with Amundsen were Olav Bjaaland, Helmer Hanssen,

Amundsen and members of his South Pole exploration party

Svene Hassel, and Oscar Wisting. Their joy was subdued, and there was no cheering or uncontrollable excitement. Instead, they all shook hands as Amundsen unfurled a Norwegian flag. Together, with each man's hand on the pole, they planted the Norwegian flag into the snow. Amundsen spoke these words: "So we plant you, dear flag, on the South Pole, and give the plain on which it lies the name King Haakon VII's Plateau." All that remained for the moment was to record the event with photographs. Both Amundsen and Bjaaland took photos, but it was Bjaaland's snapshot camera that provided the historic record. Amundsen's camera had been damaged during the trip and his photos were lost.

Haakon VII of Norway

Bjaaland's photograph of Amundsen and the three other members of the party at the South Pole

In all, Amundsen and his men would spend three days at the South Pole. Their time was mainly spent in making calculations of their geographical position. They knew that they had not found the pole's exact point, 90 degrees south, but they knew they were very close. To assure that they had actually crossed the South Pole, Amundsen had Wisting and Hassel ski out 10 miles (16 kilometers) in four different directions at right angles to one another. This was to assure that they had made no mistakes and had achieved the actual pole. Amundsen was well aware of the controversy over Cook's and Peary's claims to the North Pole, and he did not want the same dispute with Scott. He took the greatest care to prove that he had indeed reached the South Pole.

Amundsen named his South Pole camp Polheim. There he left a small tent containing letters to Scott and to the King of Norway. In his note, he asked Scott to deliver the king's letter for him as a confirmation of his claim in case Amundsen did not make it back. As an added precaution, Amundsen had his men set out four black flags in a box pattern at a distance of 10 miles (16 kilometers) from the camp. Attached to each flag was a bag containing a note that would help Scott find his South Pole camp. Without confirmation by Scott, Amundsen's claim could be disputed. Although Amundsen and Scott were fierce competitors, they respected each other enough to accept defeat and support the winner's claim. Upon his later arrival at the Pole, Scott confirmed Amundsen's position calculations and returned with the letters in hand. It was perhaps the highest honor Scott could pay Amundsen for his achievement.

After the final calculations were made, Amundsen

Amundsen using his sextant to determine the exact position of the South Pole

realized they had missed the actual South Pole by 5.5 miles (8.9 kilometers), but this was well within the area they had marked off. By now he knew where the actual spot was, and on December 17 they set off for it. Amundsen gave the honor of first standing on the actual pole to his best skier, Olav Bjaaland. He felt that, without the benefit of skis, they would never have made it. It was therefore fitting that the honor go to the man who best represented Norwegian skiing. The pole was reached at last, and all four navigators took additional readings and confirmed the accuracy of their position. Each signed the navigation book as final proof of their achievement. Now all that was left was to return home and announce it to the world. The South Pole had been officially conquered.

Late in the evening of January 17, Amundsen and his men turned north to begin the return trip to Framheim. They saluted the Norwegian flag flying from the top of the tent, and off they went. With the strong southern wind now at their backs, sails were rigged to the sledges to give them added speed. It was Amundsen's plan to cover 15 miles (24 kilometers) per day and get up to sixteen hours of rest per day. He wanted to assure the safe return of his men. They certainly had plenty of food. The men actually gained weight on the return trip. Amundsen's planning had paid off. Sadly, at the same time, Scott's men were starving and still on their way to the pole.

On January 1, 1912, the two expeditions passed each other about 100 miles (161 kilometers) apart. The difference was that Amundsen was heading north and home, while Scott was still struggling south. The return trip for Amundsen was by no means easy, but they moved along well. The most dangerous part of the return trip was the descent from the plateau down on to the Ross Ice Shelf. Due to navigation problems, Amundsen was lost on a glacier for a while, but luck was with him, and they emerged safely from the glacier. From there on, Amundsen gave up his original plan of making 15 miles (24 kilometers) a day. Instead, he let the dog teams go for as long as they could without injuring themselves.

On January 25, 1912, Amundsen and his men, along with eleven dogs, returned to Framheim in perfect health. Scott, on the other hand, had just reached the pole on January 17, and was now heading home in terrible condition. Amundsen was clearly the victor, and as his men rejoiced, he could only hope that Scott would return safely.

Amundsen on skis

The *Fram* left the Bay of Whales one week after Amundsen's return. There was no need to remain longer. The most important thing now was to reach civilization and announce their success. Soon the *Fram* sailed into a harbor on Tasmania, an island southeast of Australia. The first question Amundsen asked was for news of Scott. He was both pleased and puzzled to learn that no word of Scott had been received. Then Amundsen sent cables to his brother Leon, King Haakon, and Don Pedro Christophersen with news of his success. Leon announced the news to the world, and the newspapers proclaimed that "the whole world has now been discovered." Amundsen was a hero. But more important to Amundsen was the fact that he had succeeded in doing what he set out to do. That was reward enough.

Amundsen's party on their trek back from the South Pole

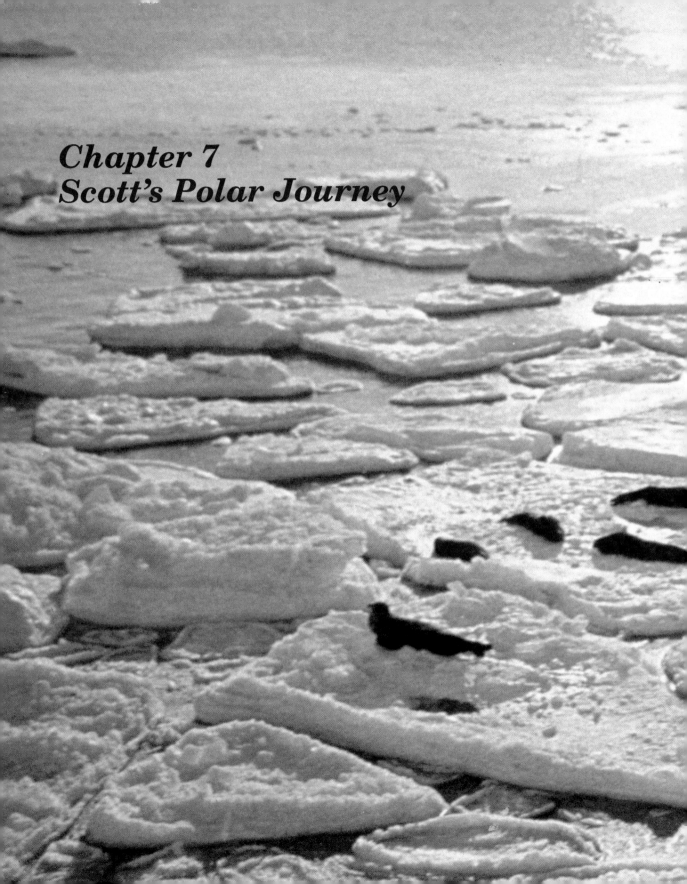

Chapter 7
Scott's Polar Journey

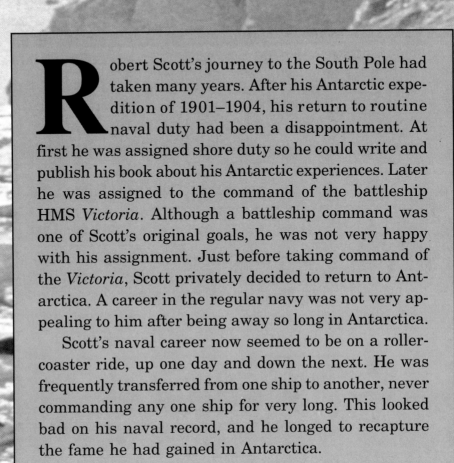

Robert Scott's journey to the South Pole had taken many years. After his Antarctic expedition of 1901–1904, his return to routine naval duty had been a disappointment. At first he was assigned shore duty so he could write and publish his book about his Antarctic experiences. Later he was assigned to the command of the battleship HMS *Victoria*. Although a battleship command was one of Scott's original goals, he was not very happy with his assignment. Just before taking command of the *Victoria*, Scott privately decided to return to Antarctica. A career in the regular navy was not very appealing to him after being away so long in Antarctica.

Scott's naval career now seemed to be on a rollercoaster ride, up one day and down the next. He was frequently transferred from one ship to another, never commanding any one ship for very long. This looked bad on his naval record, and he longed to recapture the fame he had gained in Antarctica.

Disaster struck Scott's career in February 1907 when his ship, the HMS *Albermarle*, rammed another battleship during night maneuvers. It made matters worse that Scott was not on deck at the time of the accident. A naval board of inquiry later judged Scott innocent of charges of negligence, but he was still held responsible for leaving his post at a critical time. It was now quite clear that Scott's naval career was in serious jeopardy.

Scott's personal life was more stable. In social circles, Robert Falcon Scott was considered something of a "ladies' man," and he remained unmarried until his late thirties. Everything changed when he met Kathleen Bruce. She was a beautiful woman who enjoyed life and lived it to the fullest. She knew what she wanted from life and how to get it. Scott was ideal for her, and she had much to offer him, too.

The first meeting between Robert Scott and Kathleen Bruce took place at a luncheon in March 1906. He was very attracted by both her beauty and her intelligence. She had many qualities that Scott lacked, and he admired her style. She was also a very dominating woman, and she held visions of greatness for Scott. Scott needed her strength and greatly respected her opinions and judgment. Kathleen, on the other hand, wanted to be the wife of a national hero and to bear a hero's child. In many ways, they fulfilled each other's needs, and they were married on September 2, 1908. One year later, their son Peter was born. After that, a second Antarctic expedition would be the focus of their thoughts.

In his book, *The Voyage of Discovery*, Scott clearly challenged Shackleton to prove himself the better Antarctic explorer, and Shackleton accepted. Shackle-

Shackleton (second from left) and his party on the Nimrod

ton was angered by Scott's book. He felt that it did not give him enough credit for his part in the expedition. Shackleton intended to prove Scott's evaluation wrong by leading his own expedition to Antarctica. Feelings between them became very competitive.

In 1907, Shackleton departed for Antarctica on the *Nimrod*. His goal was to reach the South Pole, and this disturbed Scott. Scott even declared that a certain area at the edge of the Ross Ice Shelf was his own, and off-limits to Shackleton. Scott insisted that Shackleton sign an agreement that he would keep away from the area. Although Shackleton had no legal reason to agree to this, he accepted Scott's conditions. Scott, meanwhile, was going ahead with his own plans for a return to Antarctica. He could only hope that Shackleton did not make it to the pole ahead of him.

The Nimrod *makes its way through the pack ice of the Ross Sea.*

Ernest Shackleton sailed for Antarctica on August 7, 1907, with a carefully prepared plan for reaching the South Pole. At this point, there was nothing Scott could do but wait for word of Shackleton. Much to Scott's delight, Shackleton did not reach the pole. He got within 97 miles (156 kilometers) of it before being forced back by exhaustion. He did not want to endanger the lives of his men. Yet, even without reaching the pole, the expedition proved to be a great success. The explorers covered over 1,000 miles (1,609 kilometers) of new land, located the south magnetic pole, and gathered a great deal of scientific data. Shackleton returned to a hero's welcome and received worldwide acclaim. This was far different from the return of the *Discovery* in 1904, and Scott was envious of Shackleton's success.

From 1906 through 1908, Scott slowly moved ahead with his plans for a second Antarctic expedition. His main concern was to develop another means of transportation across the ice. By now, he firmly believed that dogs were not useful in Antarctica. Instead, he planned to use either ponies or motorized sledges. Scott closely followed the development of motorized vehicles and studied their potential for use in Antarctica. He was convinced that, with modern technology, he could get to the pole, and he was determined to have the newest and best equipment. But once again, he had a difficult time getting money for his expedition. Shackleton's recent trip had overshadowed Scott's *Discovery* expedition. People were not eager to support another venture that would only duplicate Shackleton's efforts. This upset Scott terribly.

It took a great deal of financial backing to purchase equipment and supplies for Scott's Antarctic expedition (above).

95

Although Scott's plans were proceeding slowly, his project was very popular with the public. After he announced his plans for the expedition, over eight thousand men came forward to volunteer for it. Great hope and excitement surrounded Scott's second expedition, and things were finally looking bright.

Scott's second expedition would center around exploration and science. He would use the *Terra Nova*, one of the relief ships that had come for him back in 1904. Right from the start, the *Terra Nova* proved inadequate for the trip. It quickly became overloaded by all the supplies, animals, and equipment being taken south. Aside from a large crew, Scott had Siberian sled dogs, Manchurian ponies, and motorized sledges on board. It would be a very long and crowded voyage to Antarctica.

The crew he selected for the expedition was very good. Among the naval officers he selected were lieutenants Henry Bowers and Victor Campbell, two very competent men. Captain Titus Oates would be in charge of the Manchurian ponies that were to pull the sledges. Three of the seamen chosen were veterans of the *Discovery* expedition: Edgar Evans, William Lashly, and Tom Crean. The scientists aboard were Edward Wilson, a doctor, artist, and zoologist; Apsley Cherry-Garrard, a zoologist; and Raymond Priestley, a geologist. These men, along with the other hand-picked crew members, made a very good team. Everything considered, the expedition should have been extremely successful.

The *Terra Nova* and its crew set sail for Antarctica on June 15, 1910. They made their first stop in New Zealand to take on additional supplies. During the voyage between New Zealand and Antarctica, they

The Terra Nova *at Cape Evans*

ran into severe storms. Three ponies were washed overboard and considerable damage was done to the ship, but they made it through.

Upon their arrival on the Antarctic coast, Scott made his headquarters at a point he would later name Cape Evans. Hut Point, his old winter quarters, would be used as a second base. From here Scott would plan two major explorations. One would conduct geological studies along the coastal mountains, and the other would head for the South Pole.

Setting up supply depots

First, they had to set up a series of supply depots along the route to the pole. It would be extremely hard work, but it was necessary if they were to succeed. Shackleton did this on his polar expedition, and it had saved his life. Scott planned to follow Shackleton's example, but he meant to cover those last 97 miles (156 kilometers) to the pole, too.

As on Scott's *Discovery* expedition, things began to go wrong from the start. One of the three motor sledges fell through the ice as it was being unloaded, and it was lost. The remaining two were constantly breaking down and were not very useful. Scott's attempt to replace the dog teams was also a failure. He tried to rely on ponies and man-hauling to get from place to place. Once again, dog teams proved to be the best,

Scott in his winter headquarters

but Scott was reluctant to use them. He did not want to see the dogs suffer as those on the *Discovery* expedition had. He put his faith in the ponies, but this proved to be a great mistake. The dog teams were always pulling ahead of the ponies and could do the work easily when handled correctly.

They spent their first season in Antarctica laying out the supply depots to the pole, and all was going well. One party, led by Victor Campbell, sailed along the Ross Ice Shelf and explored King Edward VII Land. As they reached the Bay of Whales, they encountered another ship. It was *Fram*, with Roald Amundsen's expedition on board. Amundsen's camp was 60 miles (97 kilometers) closer to the pole than Scott's camp. Now it was clear that the two expeditions were in a race to the South Pole.

Life around Cape Evans was anything but dull for Scott's men. In late February 1911, three men and four ponies became trapped on an ice floe that broke away from the Ross Ice Shelf. The men spent a terrifying day on the ice before they were rescued. The ponies were not as lucky, and three were lost. A second near-disaster befell Campbell's exploring party. While on a six-week geological field study, they became stranded. The men were short on food, and they did not have enough warm clothes to withstand the winter. They survived by building a snow cave shelter and then using whatever animals they could find for food. Fortunately, all six survived the long winter and made it back to camp six months later.

Scott's party left Cape Evans for the South Pole on October 24, 1911, with all the splendor of a royal send-off. Flags were flown, and the men cheered the party on. However, the joy was quickly left behind. The motorized sledges soon broke down, the weather took a turn for the worse, and the men were tent-bound for five days. They were rapidly falling behind schedule. It was now up to the ponies and the dog teams to get them as far as possible before the men had to resort to man-hauling their equipment.

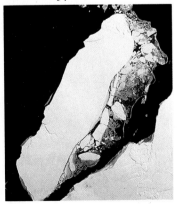

A gigantic island of ice that has broken away from the Ross Ice Shelf

To reach the South Pole, the men first had to advance up the Beardmore Glacier. In all, twelve men pulled sledges up and over the glacier's rugged ice blocks and deep crevasses. When they reached the top with their supplies, Scott sent four men back. He divided the remaining men into two teams, and the team that proved to be the strongest would go to the pole. Scott made his final decision on January 4, 1912, when he chose Wilson, Oates, Evans, and Bowers as the final team. The others would return to camp.

100

Scott's original plan was to take only three other men to the pole. All the food and fuel oil was set up for four. At the last minute he chose to take Bowers along as a fifth man. This required repacking their rations, and it cost them valuable time. In addition, Bowers had left his skis behind and was traveling on foot. This slowed everyone down. Had Scott taken three men along instead of four, the expedition would probably have ended quite differently.

This photograph of Scott's party man-hauling a sledge was found in Scott's tent after his death.

Spirits were high as the five headed south toward the pole, but their joy would be short-lived. Soon exhaustion set in, and man-hauling their sledge became torture. In their minds, the thought of losing the race to the Norwegians became stronger as they drew nearer to the pole. Their hopes of winning were shattered as they came across the tracks of Amundsen's dog teams. They knew they had lost the race, and all the hardships they had endured would only earn them second place. It was a bitter disappointment.

Scott and his party reached the South Pole on January 17, 1912. There they found a small tent, and in it was a letter from Amundsen saying he had arrived on December 14. One can only imagine the

Scott's party reaches the pole, only to find Amundsen's tent there. Left to right are Scott, Oates, Wilson, and Evans.

feelings that Scott and his men shared. Now they were faced with a journey of over 800 miles (1,287 kilometers) just to get back to their base. With only a limited amount of food on hand and no safety margin, it was a grim prospect.

The ceremonies at the South Pole lasted about a day. They took photographs, made calculations of their geographical position, and raised the British flag. On the trip home they continued to make scientific observations and to collect geological specimens. Cold, hunger, and overall weakness were taking their toll very quickly, and the men were becoming desperate. Evans was in the worst condition. He was suffering from frostbite and a gangrene infection from a small cut. He had also fallen several times and hit his head. Finally, on February 17, near the bottom of the Beardmore Glacier, he collapsed and died. Perhaps the rest knew it would be only a matter of time before they joined him, but they pushed on.

Incredibly, the remaining four managed to get off the glacier and on to the Ross Ice Shelf. The weather conditions became worse as the temperature dropped to −30 degrees Fahrenheit (−34 degrees Celsius). Titus Oates was weakening and begged the others to leave him behind, but they refused. Overcome with frostbite and exhaustion, he could no longer go on. On March 17, Oates's birthday, he crawled from the tent, saying he would be gone for some time. The others knew what would happen, but they were too weak to stop him. He never returned. The remaining three, Scott, Wilson, and Bowers, were not in much better shape, but they pressed on. They felt that if they could reach One Ton Depot, the last depot before base camp, they would survive.

The five members of Scott's expedition at the South Pole. Left to right, standing, are Oates, Scott, and Evans; seated are Bowers and Wilson.

The end for Scott came just 11 miles (18 kilometers) from One Ton Depot. They reached that point on March 21 and made their final camp. There was just enough food and fuel left to make it. However, misfortune struck again. A blizzard came up that blew for nine days, and it sealed their fate. Scott's right foot was now badly frostbitten, and he, like Oates, found he could not go on. Wilson and Bowers chose to remain with their leader. There they were found almost eight months later, when a search party reached them on November 12, 1912. The three had died side by side in their tent, frozen into their sleeping bags.

"I do not regret this journey," Scott had written in his diary, "which has shown that Englishmen can endure hardships, help one another and meet death with as great fortitude as ever in the past." In a sense, Scott achieved in death the victory he had missed at the pole.

Robert Falcon Scott was not a man who accepted defeat easily. After he realized that they probably would not make it back alive, Scott began writing a series of diary entries to explain his actions and why they were lost. Because he was a brilliant writer, he became after his death the hero he had never become in life. Scott's diary entries clearly show that he believed all his plans and preparations were the best possible and that his defeat was due to bad luck and bad weather. History now shows that it was his lack of preparation and bad judgment that led to his downfall. In many cases, he placed blame elsewhere when he was at fault. Even under the best possible conditions, Scott probably would not have beaten Amundsen to the South Pole, but with good judgment he might have returned alive.

Scott's last diary entry: "We shall stick it out to the end but we are getting weaker of course and the end cannot be far. It seems a pity but I do not think I can write more— R. Scott. Last Entry—For God's sake look after our people"

Chapter 8
Two Very Different Heroes

Two men had attempted to conquer the South Pole. Both had the ambition and courage necessary to achieve greatness. But it was Roald Amundsen who succeeded, through his determination and careful planning. Although he encountered many hardships on the way to the pole, his detailed preparations made it possible to complete the journey. Amundsen endured the same severe weather and dangerous terrain that Scott did. The difference was that Amundsen was trained for such conditions and took every possible precaution against the unexpected. Where survival was concerned, Amundsen took no risks and did not depend on luck. There lies the difference between success and failure. Scott relied too much on luck, and it failed him. Yet, ironically, Scott would be the one whom history remembered best.

The success of Roald Amundsen's expedition made headline news around the world. He would be proclaimed as the greatest explorer of his day, but his fame would be short-lived. When Amundsen published the report of his expedition, it made very dry reading. His style was to report facts and not dramatize his accomplishments. When he gave lectures it was the same. Audiences applauded his achievement, but they were not moved by his presentation. Amundsen had a difficult time keeping the public excited about his South Pole conquest. People soon lost sight of him as the newspaper articles faded, and he became a forgotten hero to most of the world.

In a way, Robert Falcon Scott emerged as the victor of the South Pole. This was largely because of the dramatic way in which he died. When the search party finally located Scott and his companions, they carefully recorded the manner in which they were found. Every detail was noted and Scott's diary, along with letters written by Bowers and Wilson, were brought back and made public. In death, Scott was made larger than life.

Scott's wife and several of his sponsors carefully went over his notes and his diary, changing many statements that would make him look bad. The reports that were eventually made public showed Scott as a true hero and competent leader who fell on bad luck. His actions and his noble acceptance of death were presented in the highest tradition of the Royal Navy. Scott's last days were presented in such a manner that they would inspire people to endure hardships and suffering in the true "British" manner. Supreme self-sacrifice was demonstrated by their continuing to collect geological specimens right up to the

Amundsen honored in a parade in Oslo, Norway

end, even after they realized they might never make it back. Such is the stuff that legends are made of, and in death, Scott became a legendary hero that generations of British school children would admire.

After his polar conquest, things were very different for Roald Amundsen. He was on tour in America when the news of Scott's death reached him. Amundsen was quoted as saying, "I would gladly forego any honor or money, if thereby I could have saved Scott his terrible death." Amundsen's grief over Scott's death was sincere. No matter how strong the competition was between these two men, they understood each other. They shared the same goals and suffered the same hardships to achieve them. Amundsen fully understood what happened to Scott, and he deeply regretted that he had not been able to save him.

When British newspapers got word of Scott's tragic end, they went so far as to call Amundsen lucky in his success and indirectly responsible for Scott's death. The press felt that if Scott had not been beaten to the pole, his joy of success would have carried him home safely. In reality, even if Scott had been the first to reach the pole, he may still have died on the way back. The criticisms of Amundsen were totally unfair, and they hurt him deeply. It was as if Amundsen were

Amundsen in 1920

being blamed instead of honored for winning the race to the pole. This affected him in later life, as he tried to recapture the glory that Scott's death had stolen from him.

A monument erected in London, England, to honor Robert Scott

Perhaps it was all the controversy about Scott's death that caused Amundsen to give up exploration. After all, his dash to the South Pole was supposed to be a short diversion before beginning his real goal of drifting across the North Pole. Adding to Amundsen's problem was the debt that his expedition has accumulated. Heroes cannot escape their debtors, and Amundsen was no exception. He canceled plans for the Arctic expedition and worked hard to pay off his debts. After World War I began in 1914, the world's attention was no longer focused on exploration. Amundsen was slowly slipping from the public eye, and he sought a new means to recapture his past glory. He was not a man who could live on his past achievements. He needed new worlds to conquer.

Aviation was to be Amundsen's new frontier. He first watched an airplane flight in 1913, and he began flying lessons in 1914. Amundsen received the first civilian pilot's license in Norway. On his early flights he tried to set some records, but they all failed and the press criticized him severely. Amundsen truly became a fallen hero.

He was back in action in 1925, however, when he joined with a wealthy American named Lincoln Ellsworth in an attempt to fly over the North Pole. This ill-planned venture nearly cost them their lives. The two crashed on the way to the pole, yet they did set a record for flying the farthest north. Amundsen was once again popular, and the story of their heroic escape from death was a triumph.

111

In 1926, Amundsen and Ellsworth made another attempt to fly to the North Pole, this time in the *Norge*. This was a dirigible, or blimp, known at the time as an airship. As they were preparing for their flight, explorer Richard E. Byrd flew an airplane to the North Pole and snatched that achievement from them. In spite of Byrd's victory, the *Norge* took off and became the first airship to fly over the North Pole. After this success, Amundsen intended to retire with honor. But controversy continued to follow Amundsen. A bitter feud broke out between Amundsen and Umberto Nobile, the designer and pilot of the *Norge*. Nobile claimed that Amundsen received too much credit for their success and that the honor was rightfully his. The feud became public, and it did no good for Amundsen's image. This, combined with the fact that creditors were still pursuing him, made Amundsen a very bitter man.

Amundsen had been officially retired for two years when, in May 1928, he received word that Umberto Nobile, in the airship *Italia*, disappeared on a flight to the North Pole. Norway offered to organize a rescue party headed by Amundsen, but the Italian dictator, Benito Mussolini, flatly refused. He too was bitter over the feud between Amundsen and Nobile. Norway went ahead with the rescue plan, but quietly dropped Amundsen from command. Amundsen was furious and began to organize his own expedition. He felt it was his duty to try and save a fellow explorer, even if that explorer was not a friend.

Amundsen's rescue operation consisted of a flying boat and crew provided by the French government. They would join the twenty aircraft and ships that were already searching for Nobile. It soon became a

Italian dictator Benito Mussolini

112

race to see who would find Nobile first. Putting caution aside for the first time in his life, Amundsen took off on June 18, 1928, to find Nobile. Shortly after takeoff, Amundsen's plane disappeared from sight and was never seen again. Several months later, wreckage from the plane was found. It was clear that those aboard had survived the crash but lost their fight for survival. Nobile was eventually rescued, but Amundsen was dead. In death, Amundsen returned to the Polar Sea where his career began. It was a fitting end for one of the greatest explorers of all times.

Amundsen at the doorway of the Norge before taking off on his flight over the North Pole

113

Epilogue

Men like Amundsen and Scott left a great legacy for today's scientists and explorers. They truly broke the frontiers of exploration and showed others the way. Our present-day flights to the moon and beyond are really not that different from voyages of the *Discovery* or the *Fram*. Success still depends on dedication, courage, and good preparation.

The expeditions of Amundsen and Scott showed scientists the right and wrong ways of living and working in Antarctica. The lessons they learned have saved many lives. They have also provided a better understanding of Antarctica and of our planet as a whole. Modern-day explorers now go into the Antarctic with tents designed by Scott, the now-traditional Scott tents. Sledges designed by Nansen and Amundsen are still used, but pulled by snowmobiles, the motorized sledges envisioned by Scott. Everywhere we look in the polar sciences today, we see the handiwork of Amundsen, Scott, Shackleton, or Nansen. We owe much to the founders of polar exploration.

In the world of science and exploration, the names of Amundsen and Scott are still remembered. The present-day South Pole Station, operated by the United States' National Science Foundation, bears the name Amundsen-Scott Station. It stands as a reminder of, and a tribute to, these explorers who first set foot on the South Pole. With his triumph at the pole, Amundsen demonstrated the value of careful planning and determination. Scott, on the other hand, showed the true character of an explorer by carrying back with him the evidence of Amundsen's success. His eventual

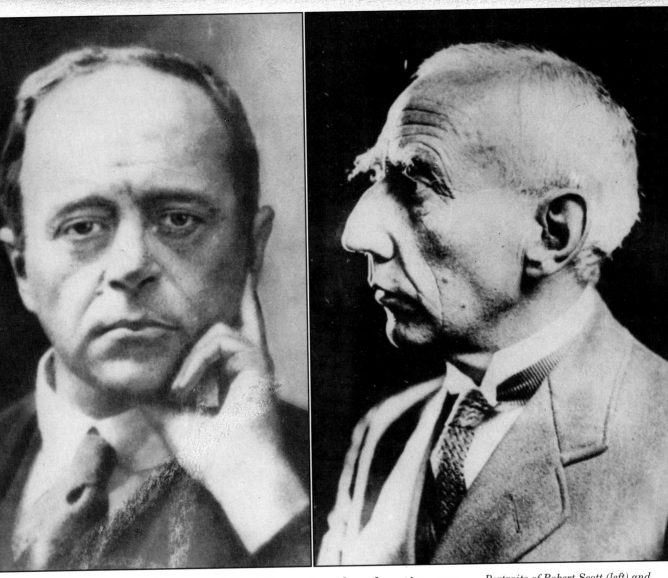

death clearly showed that the price of exploration can be high, but the risk must be taken if we are to advance human knowledge. In 1986, seven astronauts lost their lives as the space shuttle *Challenger* exploded during lift-off. These seven brave explorers were living the tradition established by Amundsen and Scott; they gave up their lives for a mission they believed in. Their example will live on for future explorers as humanity continues to push back the frontiers of deep oceans and boundless space.

Portraits of Robert Scott (left) and Roald Amundsen (right)

Appendices

Scott's Miserable Arrival at the South Pole

On January 17, 1912, after reaching the South Pole, Scott made the following entry in his diary:

> The Pole. Yes, but under very different circumstances from those expected. We have had a horrible day—add to our disappointment a head wind 4 to 5, with a temperature −22 degrees, and companions labouring on with cold feet and hands. . . . Great God! this is an awful place and terrible enough for us to have laboured to it without the reward of priority.

After reaching the pole on December 14, 1911, Amundsen left a note to Scott and a letter to King Haakon VII of Norway. Here is his note to Scott:

Dear Captain Scott,

As you probably are the first to reach this area after us, I will ask you kindly to forward this letter to King Haakon VII. If you can use any of the articles left in the tent please do not hesitate to do so. With kind regards I wish you a safe return.

Yours truly,
Roald Amundsen

Opposite page: Antarctic iceberg at sunset

Tins and packages of food that are still on the shelves in Scott's hut

What Do Polar Explorers Eat?

Daily rations for Scott's men

Tea—.7 ounces (20 grams)
Biscuits—1 pound (454 grams)
Cocoa—.85 ounces (24 grams)
Pemmican—12 ounces
    (340 grams)
Butter—2 ounces (56.75 grams)
Sugar—3 ounces (85.13 grams)
Total—about 2 pounds, 3 ounces
    (980 grams)
Total calories—4,430 per day

Daily rations for Amundsen's men

Biscuits—14 ounces (400 grams)
Dried milk—2.6 ounces
    (75 grams)
Chocolate—4.4 ounces
    (125 grams)
Pemmican—13 ounces
    (375 grams)
Total—about 2 pounds, 2 ounces
    (975 grams)
Total calories—4,560 per day

Some of the basic nutrients provided by the rations:

Scott's rations:
Thiamine—1.26 mg.
Riboflavin—1.65 mg.
Nicotinic acid—18.18 mg.

Needed for working at 4,500 calories a day:

Thiamine—1.8 mg.
Riboflavin—2.4 mg.
Nicotinic acid—29.7 mg.

Thiamine (vitamin B_1) is found in meats, whole-grain bread and cereal, nuts, potatoes, and most green vegetables. Thiamine deficiency leads to beriberi, a disease of the nervous system.

Riboflavin (vitamin B_2), is found in milk, cheese, liver, fish, poultry, and green vegetables. It promotes growth and makes the skin and eyes healthy.

Nicotinic acid (niacin) is found in fish, green vegetables, lean meat, poultry, and whole-grain cereal and bread. It promotes growth, keeps tissues healthy, and helps prevent pellagra.

Timeline of Events in Amundsen's and Scott's Lifetimes

1868—Robert Falcon Scott is born on June 6 near Plymouth, England

1872—Roald Engebreth Gravning Amundsen is born on July 16 in the district of Borge, now in Norway but at the time a part of Sweden

1894—Amundsen and his brother make an expedition on skis into the mountains west of Oslo

1897—Amundsen embarks on an Antarctic expedition in the *Belgica*

1901—Scott, sailing in the *Discovery*, embarks on his first Antarctic expedition

1903—Sailing in the *Gjoa*, Amundsen begins his navigation of the Northwest Passage

1904—Scott returns from the Antarctic

1905—Amundsen completes his navigation of the Northwest Passage from the North Atlantic Ocean through the Arctic Ocean to the Bering Sea

1908—Scott marries artist Kathleen Bruce

1909—Antarctic explorer Ernest Shackleton comes within 97 miles (156 kilometers) of the South Pole; Robert Peary reaches the North Pole

1910—Scott begins his second trip to Antarctica, traveling in the *Terra Nova*

1911—On December 14, Amundsen becomes the first to reach the South Pole

1912—On January 17, five weeks after Amundsen, Scott and four other expedition members arrive at the South Pole; all die on the trip back

1918—Amundsen begins an Arctic expedition, hoping to float over the North Pole in his ship *Maud*

1925—With Lincoln Ellsworth, Amundsen unsuccessfully attempts to fly over the North Pole

1926—Americans Richard Byrd and Floyd Bennett fly a Fokker airplane over the North Pole; with Lincoln Ellsworth and Umberto Nobile, Amundsen flies the dirigible *Norge* over the North Pole

1928—Amundsen dies in the Arctic while leading a search party for Umberto Nobile

Glossary of Terms

admiralty—A government department in charge of naval and maritime affairs

caribou—A large North American deer related to the reindeer

constellation—A group of stars that appear to form the outline of a certain pattern

crevasse—A deep crack in glacial ice or in snow

expedition—A journey taken for a specific purpose, such as discovery or scientific research

fjord—A narrow channel of water between steep cliffs; actually a glacial valley filled with sea water

geographic pole—The point where the earth's lines of longitude come together

geology—The study of the earth's history as recorded in rocks and minerals

hemisphere—Half of a sphere, such as the earth; the earth is divided into northern and southern hemispheres by the equator and into eastern and western hemispheres by lines of longitude

ice floe—A large, thin, flat mass of coastal ice floating in the sea

magnetic pole—The spot toward which magnetic compasses point

man-haul—To pull a load by human power, rather than by using animals or machines

marooned—Left ashore in a desolate region

midshipman—A student who is attending a naval academy to train for a commission in the navy

pack ice—Thick masses of ice formed when ice floes push together in the sea

plateau—A flat-surfaced land area that stands high above surrounding land

port-of-call—A port in the course of a voyage, where a ship may get repairs or take on extra supplies, cargo, or fuel

scurvy—A disease caused by lack of vitamin C

sledge—A sled-like vehicle for carrying loads over snow or ice

Bibliography

For further reading, see:

Brewster, Barney. *Antarctica: Wilderness at Risk.* Brick House Publishing Co. Andover, MA: 1982.

Cameron, Ian. *Antarctica, the Last Continent.* Little, Brown and Company. Boston: 1974.

Chapman, Walker. *The Loneliest Continent.* New York Graphic Society Publishers, Ltd. Greenwich, CT: 1964.

Cherry-Garrard, Apsley. *The Worst Journey in the World.* Chatto and Windus. London: 1965.

Honnywill, Eleanor. *The Challenge of Antarctica.* Nelson. Oswestry, Shropshire, England: 1984.

Huntford, Roland. *The Last Place on Earth.* Athenaeum. New York: 1986.

Lewis, Richard S. *A Continent for Science.* Viking. New York: 1965.

Seaver, George. *Edward Wilson of the Antarctic.* Murray. London: 1933.

Index

Page numbers in boldface type indicate illustrations.

Picture Identifications for Chapter Opening Spreads

6–7—Paradise Bay, Antarctica
16–17—Waterfront fish market in Bergen, Norway
26–27—Iceberg in Gerlache Strait, Brabant Island, Antarctica
44–45—Harbor near the British port city of Plymouth
58–59—Coastal ice floes off the Antarctic coast
72–73—Antarctica: sunset over the icebergs
90–91—"Pancake" ice floes in Antarctic waters
106–107—Unusual ice shapes formed by pressure

Picture Acknowledgements

About the Author

Paul P. Sipiera is a professor of Earth Sciences at William Rainey Harper College in Palatine, Illinois. His principal areas of research are the study of meteorites and volcanic rocks. In 1983-1984, he spent over five weeks living and working on the Polar Plateau as part of the National Science Foundation's Antarctic Search for Meteorites Project. He returned in 1985-1986 to observe penguins and examine rock formations on the Antarctic peninsula. Besides participating in the United States Antarctic Research Program, he is a member of the Explorers Club. When he is not studying science, Sipiera can be found traveling the world or working on his farm in Galena, Illinois.